ENJOYING
the
BIBLE

ENJOYING

the

BIBLE

LITERARY APPROACHES TO
LOVING THE SCRIPTURES

MATTHEW MULLINS

Baker Academic
a division of Baker Publishing Group
Grand Rapids, Michigan

© 2021 by Matthew Mullins

Published by Baker Academic
a division of Baker Publishing Group
PO Box 6287, Grand Rapids, MI 49516-6287
www.bakeracademic.com

Printed in the United States of America

Library of Congress Cataloging-in-Publication Data
Names: Mullins, Matthew, 1983– author.
Title: Enjoying the Bible : literary approaches to loving the scriptures / Matthew Mullins.
Description: Grand Rapids, Michigan : Baker Academic, a division of Baker Publishing Group, 2021. | Includes bibliographical references and index.
Identifiers: LCCN 2020027152 | ISBN 9781540961662 (paperback) | ISBN 9781540963932 (casebound)
Subjects: LCSH: Bible—Appreciation. | Bible—Criticism, interpretation, etc.
Classification: LCC BS538.5 .M85 2021 | DDC 220.6/6—dc23
LC record available at https://lccn.loc.gov/2020027152

Baker Publishing Group publications use paper produced from sustainable forestry practices and post-consumer waste whenever possible.

21 22 23 24 25 26 27   8 7 6 5 4 3 2

For Michael Travers and Tom Lisk
meliores doctores

Contents

Preface

Throughout the year and a half or so in which I worked on this book in earnest, friends, colleagues, and students who knew I was writing about the Bible and poetry would frequently ask me a question that went something like this: "So, how's the Psalms book coming?" The first few times, I tried to explain that it wasn't really a book about the Psalms but a book about how the Psalms remind us that understanding the Bible requires more than one kind of reading. Eventually, I gave up on reframing the question and would simply offer an update on my progress. I begin with this anecdote to dispel any notion readers may have that this is a book about the Psalms. While I will spend a good bit of time referencing and analyzing various psalms, my interest in poetry here is not merely an interest in the actual poems found in the Bible. In short, this book is about the pleasure of understanding. By that I mean two things. First, I mean that understanding what we read can be pleasurable. But second, I mean that, sometimes, you must take pleasure in something *in order to understand it.*

I said that I worked on the book in earnest for about a year and a half, but I've been writing it in my head, in my class lectures, and in my conversations with students and colleagues for at least half a dozen years. I teach at a confessional liberal arts college housed at a Southern Baptist seminary. Many of my students have been reading, studying, even teaching the Bible from a young age. They have listened to countless sermons and devotions. Most can probably recite the names of the books of the Bible in canonical order and can quote many individual verses from memory. My students, in other words, are not typically novice Bible readers. And yet, when they show up in my survey of American literature and pick up their first poems by Anne Bradstreet or Phillis Wheatley, I hear the same protestations year after year:

> Why doesn't the author just come right out and say what she means?
>
> What's she *really* trying to say?
>
> It seems like she's making it difficult to understand on purpose.
>
> If *that's* what the poem's about, then why isn't that idea in the title?
>
> Okay, okay, but what's the point?

My students, like most people, expect poetry to function like explanatory prose, perhaps because both take the form of printed words on paper. The problem is that poetry is not usually trying to explain an idea. It has a different purpose, which is why the writer chose to write a poem rather than a sermon, speech, or research essay.

The longer I've taught poetry in this Christian context, the more I've become aware of how rare it is to have a student who truly enjoys poems, and rarer still that I encounter a student who knows how to read them well. And then one day it dawned on me that if most of my students, self-proclaimed lovers of the Bible, do not know what to do with poems, then it would follow that most of them would not know what to do with a significant portion of the Scriptures. And yet, they did not seem to struggle with the Bible in the same way they struggled with the poetry in my literature classes. To me, this was dissonant, or, as I more likely thought of it, weird. If you had no problem reading John Winthrop's sermon "A Model of Christian Charity" but couldn't feel the vulnerability in Bradstreet's poem "The Author to Her Book," it was evident to me that you were equipped to read the sermon but not the poem. If that was the case, then why wouldn't you experience the same disconnect when going from Paul's Letter to the Ephesians to David's psalms of lament? There were two possible answers: either students were struggling to apply principles of reading biblical poetry to nonbiblical poems, or they were not reading the poetry of the Bible as poetry. For a number of reasons, I concluded the second was the more likely answer.

When reading the Bible, my students approached everything in the book as if it were explanatory prose. They would ask the same questions of Psalm 23 as they would of Ephesians 1. They would look for the main idea and try to draw an application for their own lives out of that main idea. Of course, they didn't come up with this approach or with this idea of what the Bible is on their own. They were taught this way of reading implicitly and explicitly over the course of their lives. I slowly began to realize just how thoroughly most Christians thought of the Bible itself as an instruction manual and of reading it as a process of looking for instruction or information. This revelation was personal as well. I recognized a deep divide in my own reading life between the works of literature I spend so much time with and the Bible. The problem with this dissonance is that the Bible is not only an instruction manual. It is so much more. Thus, to read it always for information is to miss out on the other forms of meaning it has for us, most especially the kind of relationship with God it seeks to foster.

The basic argument of this book is that much of the Bible is written to be enjoyed. The implication is that if reading the Bible does not enact pleasure in you, then you may not understand what you have read. By "understand" here I don't mean that you simply realize you *should* be comforted as a result of reading Psalm 23. I mean that the act of reading Psalm 23 should literally make you feel comforted. The Bible is our most direct access to God's words—it was written not only to convey information about him but also to provide a way for us to commune with him, to meet him in his Word. But in a world that largely separates information from enjoyment, we've come to experience the Bible primarily as a textbook or handbook, missing out on many of its more pleasurable aspects. The result is that we don't always love it like we could, or through it love God as we should.

Therefore, this book has two purposes. First, it seeks to change the way we think about the Bible itself as a text, to expand our sense of it from instruction manual to work of literary art. Second, it attempts to teach us how to read the Bible as a work of literary art. These purposes presuppose a radical assumption: that understanding what we read is not merely an intellectual exercise, and so we need more than our brains to understand the Bible. Because of their appeal to our emotions and imaginations, works of literature offer excellent models of texts that require a more comprehensive mode of reading. So the argument and purposes of the book come together in its method, which is to teach us how to think about and read literature in an effort to revolutionize our reading of the Bible. In other words, if you can learn how to enjoy a poem by Robert Frost, you're more likely to enjoy the Scriptures. And my prayer is that if you can learn to enjoy the Scriptures, then you will come to love them like you love other things: good food, your favorite film, a binge-worthy show. Just imagine if you delighted in the Bible like you delight in those things . . .

A quick note about the literary examples you'll find throughout the book: Because I am a professor of American literature, most of the poems we'll practice reading come from the American literary tradition. I was also trying to keep the cost of permissions down, and so nearly all the poems are old enough to be in the public domain. Ultimately, I think this works out well, because these poems will likely not be as far removed in time and culture as the Bible from many of my readers, but there will still be some distance, so they offer a kind of half step in terms of familiarity. In other words, we will practice reading literature via texts that are somewhat alien to us as we step toward reading the Bible, a text far removed from us in time and culture. My hope is that there will be an added benefit of possibly encountering some poets and poems you may not be familiar with.

A word about language: I am not a Bible scholar. When I talk about the Bible and its form, I am (almost) always talking about an English translation of the Bible. (I use the NIV translation throughout, unless otherwise noted, and I sometimes reference scholars who are working with the original languages.) The act of translating from one language to another is always also an act of interpretation. I don't mention this to suggest that those of us able to read the Bible only in languages other than Hebrew, Aramaic, or Greek are not *really* reading it. But I do want to call attention to the mediated nature of our reading. We are relying on the linguistic, historical, literary, and philosophical expertise *and* wisdom of the translators. If God were to speak to me in Hebrew, I would not understand. I don't speak Hebrew. I am thankful that the Bible has been translated into my language so that I can meet God in his Word, but I also acknowledge that the elements of form that are so integral to understanding a work of literature are unavoidably different in English than in Hebrew. On some level, a philologist could help us think through the complexities of translation, but on another level, there will always remain something of a mystery in this phenomenon. For the sake of this book, I hope you will be able to learn from the principles examined, though I will be talking about the Bible as I know it in English.

I pray that this book will help you come to love the Scriptures like you love your favorite songs. In that spirit, and inspired by James K. A. Smith, I want to close these prefatory remarks by sharing an abridged playlist of the music that was running in the background in my office as I wrote, on the couch as I read, in the kitchen as I cleaned up (and occasionally cooked), and in the backyard as I weeded the garden and played with my kids throughout the time I worked on this book:

Gregory Alan Isakov, "The Stable Song"
Gillian Welch, "Look at Miss Ohio"
Aretha Franklin, "Ain't No Way"
Pedro the Lion, "Yellow Bike"
Josh Garrels, "At the Table"
Al Green, "Love and Happiness"
Sho Baraka, "Love, 1959"
Willie Nelson, "Hello Walls"
Iron & Wine, "Call It Dreaming"
Otis Redding, "That's How Strong My Love Is"
The Avett Brothers, "No Hard Feelings"
Jason Isbell, "If It Takes a Lifetime"
CHVRCHES, "Get Out"
Bon Iver, "8(circle)"

Jackie Hill Perry, "Better"
Daniel Norgren, "My Rock Is Crumbling"
Kacey Musgraves, "Happy & Sad"
Josh Ritter, "When Will I Be Changed"
TW Walsh, "Fundamental Ground"
Mandolin Orange, "Wildfire"

An early working title of this project was *You Can't Understand the Bible If You Don't Love Literature.* May this book be a joyous experience in cultivating that love and understanding.

Acknowledgments

When I reflect on the many people without whom this book would not exist, the first group that comes to mind is my students at Southeastern Baptist Theological Seminary, the College at Southeastern, and Nash Correctional Institution. These are people who want to read well, and I often feel like I could spend all day every day doing nothing else but reading with them. I am especially thankful to all those inquisitive students who have helped me refine my understanding of and experience with poetry in the many sections of the survey of American literature I have taught here since I first began as an adjunct professor in 2007.

I am grateful for my institution, our administration, and our board of trustees. Danny Akin, Ryan Hutchinson, Bruce Ashford, Scott Pace, and Keith Whitfield have created an environment in which I have been able to teach and write for my own edification, and for that of my students and peers. I am also grateful for my colleagues at Southeastern. We have a faculty whose members genuinely care for one another, and even amid the regular frustrations that are a natural part of any work environment I am constantly reminded that I am surrounded by coworkers who are also friends. During my time here I have especially benefited from the friendship of Chip Hardy, Tracy McKenzie, Stephen Eccher, Adrianne Miles, Walter Strickland, Stephen Wade, George Robinson, Ben Merkle, Miguel Echevarria, and Jake Pratt. Finally, I cannot imagine being part of a team at Southeastern that does not include Billie Goodenough. She was the first person to read every word of this book, as she has been for so much of what I have written, deleted, and published since 2012. Billie, thank you for all your help over the years.

Beyond Southeastern, Mark Rifkin told me to stop worrying about how this project would look to the academic profession and to write what I needed to write. Thanks, Mark. Josh Toth listened to a long version of this thing as we walked down a never-ending street in Heidelberg (appropriately) in the late spring of 2019. He even asked questions. Craig Morehead is the person who got me hooked on the prose works of poets, and he is also a much better thinker than I am. Belinda Walzer and Sandy Hartwiger continue to be two of my most faithful friends in the academic world. So much of my thinking on poetry was shaped years ago in conversations with Cheryl Marsh, whom I do not get to see much these days but whose friendship continues to mean a great deal to me, as does that of Rose Brister, Aaron Chandler, Scott Gibson, Alan Benson, Cindy Webb, Jacob Babb, and David Rogers. Thanks, too, to Tony Cuda at the University of North Carolina at Greensboro for a visionary class on modernist poetry sometime around 2009 and more than one helpful workshop on teaching poetry during my time in graduate school. Pastor James White of Christ Our King Community Church in Raleigh, North Carolina, has shepherded my family well, and he also took the time to read parts of this book. I learn something new every time I cross the threshold of our church or sit down for a meal with him. A special thanks to my friend and elder, Colin Adams, who helped me navigate some key questions. Who knows where I would be without Heath Thomas? He is my big brother, and I am grateful for every minute we have together. I might not have ever pitched this book to Bob Hosack and his amazing team at Baker without the encouragement of James K. A. Smith, who put in a good word. Thanks to you both and to all the good people at Baker, especially Sarah Gombis for her patience, James Korsmo for his enthusiasm and expert eye, and Paula Gibson and her team for a beautiful design. And a special thanks to Micah Mattix and Karen Swallow Prior, who supported this project from the beginning.

How does one thank one's parents and grandparents? I am alive because of Robert L. Mullins Sr., Shirley Head, Kevin Mullins, and Kelley Mullins. Any behavior that might make me resemble a decent person is attributable to these beautiful people. Mom and Dad, I love you. The same goes for Pam and Genevieve. Vince Pienski and Sandy Pienski are my second parents, and I can't envision life without them. I would not have much motivation to get up each morning if it were not for my kids, Jai and Jada. Jai and I shared an epiphanic moment talking about a Robert Frost poem during the very early stages of writing this book. I love you, buddy, and will never forget that day. Jada, I cherish our mornings on the sunroom couch saying prayers. I love you more than you know, baby. Jenny, I have asked before, but really, what would any of it matter without you? Thanks for being my partner in everything. It is a special thing to love and like the person with whom one has chosen to spend every day of one's life, and I am grateful to God that I have that in you.

Introduction

The Hatred of Poetry and Why It Matters

When was the last time you visited your local bookstore or logged in online and bought a book of poetry? When was the last time you read a poem, whether because you wanted to or because you had to? Can you name a single poet you didn't learn about in school? Regardless of where you live or where you are from, if you are anything like 93.3 percent of Americans, then the respective answers to these questions may very well be these: Never, I can't recall, and No. The "Survey on Public Participation in the Arts" found that only 6.7 percent of American adults had read poetry at least once in the past twelve months. When Christopher Ingraham reported on this statistic for the *Washington Post* in 2015, he noted that "poetry is less popular than jazz. It's less popular than dance, and only about half as popular as knitting. The only major arts category with a narrower audience than poetry is opera."[1] But even those who fall within the 6.7 percent seem to have a contentious relationship with poetry. The American poet Marianne Moore wrote a famous poem about poetry that begins with the line "I, too, dislike it."[2] Robert Alter, a well-known scholar,

---

1. Christopher Ingraham, "Poetry Is Going Extinct, Government Data Show," *Washington Post*, April 24, 2015, https://www.washingtonpost.com/news/wonk/wp/2015/04/24/poetry-is-going-extinct-government-data-show/.
2. Marianne Moore, "Poetry," in *Complete Poems* (New York: Penguin, 1994), 36.

1

wrote a book about biblical poetry hoping it "might speak to people who love poetry" but lamenting that "biblical scholars, alas, rarely fall into that category."[3] It seems just about everyone hates poetry, even those who write it and study it for a living.

This hatred is not a recent phenomenon. The Greek philosopher Aristotle wrote a short book called *Poetics* in which he defended poetry against the attacks of his teacher, Plato. Plato, perhaps the most significant figure in Western philosophy, famously condemned the poets of Athens in his book *Republic*.[4] In those days, the primary poetic form was tragedy, plays written in verse. He argued that the poets' complicated human characters and flawed gods set dangerous examples for the people. So in his theory of the ideal republic, Plato banned the poets and only allowed poetry to be written by philosophers who would promote his political agenda. Aristotle countered that the purpose of poetry is not to offer perfect models for us to emulate, nor is it to depict horrible models for us to avoid. Rather, he says the best kind of character is "the person intermediate between these," someone to whom most people can relate.[5] After all, most people are not unbelievably noble or outrageously evil. If we can recognize ourselves in a character, Aristotle reasons, then we are more likely to learn the lessons that character learns. Today, tragedy has been usurped by the lyric as the most prevalent poetic form, but the hatred of poetry persists. Just like in the days of Plato, we have our own modern-day Aristotles who defend poetry against hatred and indifference. These defenses can help us better understand why we hate poetry and why that hatred matters.

Why We Hate Poetry

In his short book *The Hatred of Poetry*, poet and novelist Ben Lerner argues that we hate poetry because it inevitably fails to accomplish

3. Robert Alter, *The Art of Biblical Poetry*, rev. ed. (New York: Basic Books, 2011), x.

4. Plato, *Republic*, in *Plato: Complete Works*, ed. John M. Cooper (Indianapolis: Hackett, 1997), 1015–26.

5. Aristotle, *Poetics*, trans. Malcolm Heath (New York: Penguin, 1996), 21.

the one thing it's supposed to do: make the ineffable, well, effable. Poetry is supposed to express the universal feelings that we just can't quite put into words. But, by definition, anything that is ineffable cannot be put into words, and so poetry always leaves us a little (or a lot) disappointed when it fails to fully express those inexpressible feelings. To make matters worse, this disappointment is personal, because, as Lerner observes, we nearly all start out as poets. We write poetry as children and are told by our teachers that we are poets and don't even know it. When we encounter poems as adults, then, we are doubly let down by their inability to do the impossible and by their reminder that we are all failed poets.[6] Add to that the suspicion of poetry dating back to Plato. Add to *that* the modern skepticism toward any work of art that might claim to speak for a universal "we" in the face of humans' diverse experiences. Now you've got quite the obstacle course to traverse if you plan to love poetry. Lerner helps us see that we hate poetry because it inevitably disappoints us.

We also hate poetry because most of us have been trained to read for information, and if that's how you approach a poem, then you will likely find that it's hard to read. I would venture that most of us don't know what poems are for. If you're looking for information when reading a poem, you will probably get frustrated and find yourself asking questions like, What is the point? or What's the author *really* trying to say? The poem itself usually tries to tell us it's doing something other than providing information by the way it's arranged on the page. All that white space should tell us that what we're reading is different from other texts that are crammed margin-to-margin or broken up by bullet points or numbers. Have you ever wondered why some people choose to write poems instead of essays, plays, novels, or reports? Do you ever stop to consider, for instance, why the apostle Paul writes a poem into a letter or breaks out into a doxology? What is it about whatever he's saying at that moment that seems to require him to change the form and style of his writing? The poet Matthew Zapruder argues that our failure to wrestle with such questions contributes to our hatred of poetry: "It

---

6. Ben Lerner, *The Hatred of Poetry* (New York: Farrar, Straus & Giroux, 2016).

seems that our inability to grasp why we are reading poetry, for reasons fundamentally different from why we read all other forms of writing, is what makes poetry hard to understand."[7] Poetry is different from other forms of writing. While poems may very well inform us, they do not appeal primarily to our heads but to our hearts. Perhaps we hate poetry because we're trying to read it just like we read other kinds of writing that are designed to accomplish very different goals.

What's important about the historical hatred of poetry is not simply that we learn to overcome this hatred but that we understand it and what it says about us as humans. In his collection of short essays, *The Book of Delights*, poet Ross Gay recalls reading a review of Lerner's *The Hatred of Poetry* by the eminent reviewer Adam Kirsch that seemed prototypical of an entire genre of poetry defenses. Gay goes on to tally the evidence for the persistence and liveliness of poetry, offering a contrary point of view:

> I live in a Midwestern college town where once a month the line into the poetry slam at a bar actually wraps around the block and inside all variety of people share their poems to an audience of a couple hundred. And a few weeks back I took a cab to Indy and my driver told me that she reads her poems at various open mics two or three times a week. And last week, also in my town, the Poet Laureate, Juan Felipe Herrera, drew an audience of about six hundred people. Not to mention, pretty much every wedding and funeral I've ever been to has included a poem. *Requires one.*[8]

Gay demonstrates that poetry is still a vital part of culture, but this doesn't necessarily dispense with the general sense of apprehension most people feel toward the form.

What's more interesting is how we can feel this reluctance and yet still be drawn to the form in venues ranging from the nightclub to the funeral service. It's that paradoxical thing Marianne Moore describes just after she confesses her hatred for poetry:

7. Matthew Zapruder, *Why Poetry* (New York: Ecco, 2017), xiv.
8. Ross Gay, *The Book of Delights: Essays* (Chapel Hill, NC: Algonquin Books, 2019), 52–53.

> Reading it, however, with a perfect contempt for it, one
> discovers that there is in
> it after all, a place for the genuine.[9]

We struggle with poetry, and yet it seems capable of embodying our feelings and thoughts in an authentic way. But what does this love/hate for poetry have to do with understanding the Bible?

So What If We Hate Poetry?

The hatred of poetry poses a unique difficulty for Christians not only because roughly one-third of the Bible is made up of poems but also because it exposes a serious problem with how we read the Bible and understand its purpose. In other words, we have both a reading problem and a hermeneutics problem. *Hermeneutics* is the technical term for the theory of interpretation. So when I say we have a reading problem and a hermeneutics problem, what I mean is that we have problems of both practice (how we read) and theory (how we understand what we are doing when we read). These two elements, practice and theory, are inseparable, but let's address the problem of theory first. The hatred of poetry is a symptom of what I would call a hermeneutics of information. Most Christians come to the Bible with the expectation that it should teach us something practical about how to live our lives as Christians. Our theory of interpretation is to try to understand the main idea in whatever text we are reading and then figure out how to apply that main idea to our own lives, or to our family, or to our church, and so on. There is nothing wrong with this hermeneutic. The problem arises when this approach governs how we read everything. To put it another way, when we operate under the implicit assumption that to understand *every* text is to grasp its ideas and apply them, then we have allowed the hermeneutics of information to become a one-size-fits-all approach that shapes the way we read everything, even texts whose purpose is not only to inform our heads but also to move our hearts. No wonder we hate poems; they're not primarily intended to convey information but to evoke emotion!

9. Moore, "Poetry," 36.

Unfortunately, in the Western world, we live in an age and a culture that tends to prioritize the head over the heart when it comes to reading and learning. Many of us live our daily lives as if we are what philosopher and theologian James K. A. Smith calls "thinking things." We imagine our minds to be "'mission control' of the human person." Smith argues that such a view "reduces human beings to brains-on-a-stick" and wonders why we constantly experience gaps between what we know and what we do if we really are thinking things.[10] If we are thinking things, then why can't we think our way out of our habits, addictions, and routines? You can tell that you have a view of humans as thinking things if you try to change your actions with information. Have you ever tried to make or break a habit by reading, listening to a sermon or lecture, or talking about it? Smith would ask, "Has all of your new knowledge and information and thinking liberated you from those habits?"[11] After all, aren't there all kinds of things you know are right but don't do, and all kinds of things you know are wrong but do anyway? Even the apostle Paul observed this in his own life: "I do not understand what I do. For what I want to do I do not do, but what I hate I do" (Rom. 7:15). Knowledge doesn't necessarily translate into action; the head doesn't always direct the heart. And yet we live our lives—and, I would add, we read the Bible—as if this were the case, as if all we need is a little more information in order to live the Christian life more fully and joyfully.

Smith describes what I am calling a hermeneutics of information as reading with "Cartesian eyes."[12] The term "Cartesian" comes from the name of René Descartes, a French philosopher of the Enlightenment most famous for his claim, "I think, therefore I am." Or, we might say, "I know I exist because I can think; my existence is based on my thinking." We inherit the view of ourselves as "thinking things," in part, from Descartes. To read with Cartesian eyes is to read with the implicit belief that what's important about whatever you're reading is how it seeks to inform you, meaning how it seeks to give you facts or information. To read with Cartesian eyes is to read looking,

10. James K. A. Smith, *You Are What You Love: The Spiritual Power of Habit* (Grand Rapids: Brazos, 2016), 3.
11. Smith, *You Are What You Love*, 6.
12. Smith, *You Are What You Love*, 6.

first and foremost, for information. To read with Cartesian eyes is to read with your head, perhaps even to the exclusion of your heart. But what if the text you're reading was designed to appeal to your heart? What if it intends for your affections to be moved first and for your mind to follow? What if understanding a text means feeling the emotions it wants to evoke? What if to "get it" means that you must delight in what you're reading? What if to understand some texts you must love them? Now we can begin to see a serious problem with a hermeneutics of information. If you read a poem merely to understand what it's about and if you miss out on how it intends for you to *feel*, then you're actually not fully understanding the poem. When we read with Cartesian eyes, we risk misunderstanding some texts dramatically—namely, those that are not primarily intended to convey facts, ideas, and information.

Now that we can see the problems in this theory of reading, let's turn to the practice of reading and how we imagine the Bible itself as a text. When we read with Cartesian eyes, the Bible becomes a mere instruction manual. The Bible certainly offers plenty of instruction, and instruction manuals are great. Many people save them for years so that they have a reference when something breaks on their car, vacuum cleaner, or refrigerator. But how often do you break these manuals out? Who truly *loves* instruction manuals? Who has a favorite instruction manual? Who curls up in bed at night with an instruction manual? They are useful, sure. We appreciate them. We may even enjoy them to the extent that they help us assemble or fix something, but do you long to read them like you long to read your favorite mystery, or like you can't wait to binge-watch the new season of your favorite show, or like you anticipate the next installment in your favorite film series? More to the point, do you love the Bible like you love those things? If not, it may very well be that your hermeneutics causes you to approach the Bible as an instruction manual rather than as a captivating narrative, a love letter, or your go-to song when you're sad or happy. At the same time, your reading practice shapes your hermeneutics. When you sit down to learn your daily lesson from the Scriptures, you are cultivating that hermeneutics of information. Your theory and practice are locked in a loop, reinforcing one another and crowding out other ways of reading.

To sum up the problems of theory and practice, a hermeneutics
of information can cause us to misunderstand texts that are not
well suited to our Cartesian eyes, and it can prevent us from loving
the Bible by allowing us to imagine it only as an instruction manual.
Just as importantly, the practice of reading for information—likely
something we don't think about consciously—has shaped our hermeneutics of information. We weren't born with Cartesian eyes; we
developed them over years of learning, listening, and reading. Like
any other habitual practice, such routines are hard to recognize and
even harder to change.

What Do We Do?

We need new reading practices and a more comprehensive hermeneutics. It's tempting to think about retraining our Cartesian eyes
as a linear process. Surely, you might think, we need to change our
minds first, and then we will read better. But as Smith has helped
us see, our practices don't always follow our theories. In reality, the
process is both recursive and progressive. Changing your concept of
understanding is like taking two steps forward and one step back. You
regularly go back to where you just were, but in the grand scheme of
things you keep moving ahead. Developing a better hermeneutics and
better reading practices is like a line that constantly circles back on
itself but continues to move forward. While the question of whether
theory or practice comes first is a chicken-egg conundrum, it helps
to recognize the power of our hermeneutics of information and to
get an idea of the more comprehensive hermeneutics we're trying to
develop. This book aims to offer new practices designed to help you
read for more than information. In the process, I also hope to expand
our hermeneutics of information to something more like what Alan
Jacobs calls a "hermeneutics of love."[13]

A hermeneutics of love is based not on a quest for the main idea
in the text but on the greatest commandments: to love the Lord your
God with all your heart, soul, mind, and strength and to love your

13. Alan Jacobs, *A Theology of Reading: The Hermeneutics of Love* (New York:
Westview, 2001).

neighbor as yourself. The purpose of our reading, and our understanding of what we read, should be filtered through the love of God and neighbor. Why should we make these commandments, rather than a search for information, the foundation for our theory of reading? According to Jacobs, such a theory is based on Jesus's astounding remark in Matthew 22 that "all the Law and the Prophets" depend on the love of God and neighbor. Jacobs notes the magnitude of this assertion by pointing out that our reading of the Scriptures presupposes this "law of love."[14] Building on Christ's injunction, he reminds us of Augustine's claim that "anyone who thinks that he has understood the divine scriptures or any part of them, but cannot by his understanding build up this double love of God and neighbor, has not yet succeeded in understanding them."[15] If your reading of the Bible does not result in greater love of God and neighbor, then you do not *understand* what you have read. We must approach the Bible with an attitude of love for God and neighbor, and the result of our reading should be evident in our love of God and neighbor. In other words, to understand what you read is to love better, and to love better is to understand what you read.

This hermeneutics of love is well suited to the Bible. Because so much of the Scripture is, itself, written to captivate, delight, entice, comfort, confound, shock, and even sicken, if we do not love to read it for these attributes, then we do not truly understand it. Or, I might say that if you don't experience delight, comfort, shock, and so on when reading a passage intended to produce those emotions in you, then you don't fully comprehend the passage. The point is not to exchange head for heart, intellect for emotion. The point is to develop a theory and practice of reading that account for both, even blurring the lines between them. There are some things you cannot understand without genuine experience and feeling. For instance, if I write out a clear and concise explanation of how to set up a tent and you are able to do it, then we know you understand what I wrote. Conversely, just because I write a powerful account of a beautiful or

14. Jacobs, *Theology of Reading*, 9–10.
15. Augustine, *On Christian Teaching*, trans. R. P. H. Green (New York: Oxford University Press, 2008), 27.

tragic moment in my life, that does not necessarily ensure that you will be able to grasp the height or depth of the experience. Someone can explain what it's like to love a child or lose a parent, but these are phenomena that must be experienced in order to be understood. The Bible communicates the full range of meanings, from the instructional to the experiential. We need a theory and practice of reading that will work for the full spectrum. Perhaps paradoxically, we need a kind of knowledge that only comes from love. This may all seem very abstract. Perhaps we should just ask: How can we develop this kind of hermeneutics, a theory and practice of reading that will help us understand and love better?

Loving Poetry to Love the Bible

This is where the hatred of poetry comes in. Poetry is the ideal form for retraining Cartesian eyes. If you can learn to love poetry, then you can come to understand the Bible much better, because to read poetry well requires us to develop that emotional/experiential end of the reading spectrum. There's also the fact that one-third of the Bible is made up of poetry, so if you learn to love poetry, then you are also learning to love a significant portion of the Bible. But it's really the broader hermeneutic development we're after in this book. The goal is to revolutionize your theory of understanding the Bible so that you can experience its full range of significance and learn to love it more.

There are many great books that can teach you a lot about the literature of the Bible in general and biblical poetry in particular. These books fall into three major categories: scholarly, practical, and devotional. The scholarly books tend to focus on histories and technicalities of form, cultural context, linguistic evolution, and the history of biblical scholarship itself.[16] The authors of these books work with the original languages and have masterful command of the historical

16. Adele Berlin, *The Dynamics of Biblical Parallelism*, rev. ed. (Grand Rapids: Eerdmans, 2008; first published 1985 by Indiana University Press [Bloomington]); F. W. Dobbs-Allsopp, *On Biblical Poetry* (New York: Oxford University Press, 2015); J. P. Fokkelman, *Reading Biblical Poetry: An Introductory Guide* (Louisville: Westminster John Knox, 2001); James Kugel, *The Idea of Biblical Poetry* (New Haven: Yale University Press, 1981).

worlds in which the poetry of the Bible was written. They engage a long tradition of scholarship and are usually in conversation with one another. That's a scholar's job, after all: to create new knowledge about important things. To understand that new knowledge typically requires an impressive knowledge base cultivated over years of study among experts in the field. Needless to say, these books are often very technical and difficult for nonspecialists to understand.

The practical books have a different purpose. Writers like Robert Alter, Tremper Longman III, and Leland Ryken set out to make the knowledge developed in the work of the scholars more accessible to nonspecialists.[17] Many figures in this category (including those mentioned above) are, themselves, scholars in various fields, but their primary goal is to reach a broader audience with the insights hard-won by scholars. If you have no pretensions to tracing Hebrew usage, unpacking the evolution of parallelism, or parsing the lexical and semantic aspects of ancient poems but want to get a feel for why an image is repeated, what parallelism is, or how grammar affects interpretation, then these books are for you.

The devotional books on biblical poetry often attend to elements of form and language gleaned from the scholarly and practical studies, but their primary purpose is to lead readers through the poetry of the Bible as a means of spiritual encounter. Michael Travers's *Encountering God in the Psalms* is an excellent book in a tradition that also includes such important figures as Dietrich Bonhoeffer and C. S. Lewis.[18] While these books may very well teach you some important things about what poetry is and how it works, they are more focused on the devotional aspects of reading biblical poetry.

This book draws on works from all three categories but belongs most squarely alongside the practical books on biblical poetry. However, it has a very different purpose from most of the practical books

17. Alter, *Art of Biblical Poetry*; Tremper Longman III, *How to Read the Psalms* (Downers Grove, IL: InterVarsity, 1988); Leland Ryken, *Words of Delight: A Literary Introduction to the Bible* (Grand Rapids: Baker, 1992).

18. Michael E. Travers, *Encountering God in the Psalms* (Grand Rapids: Kregel, 2003); Dietrich Bonhoeffer, *Psalms: The Prayer Book of the Bible* (Minneapolis: Augsburg Fortress, 1974); C. S. Lewis, *Reflections on the Psalms* (1958; repr., New York: HarperOne, 2017).

and shares with the devotional books an attention to the heart. The practical books tend to focus on making the work of biblical scholars accessible to nonscholars, and that work is usually focused on the form, content, and context of the biblical poems themselves. I am not a biblical scholar. I am a literary critic who is interested in hermeneutics. So whereas most of the practical books are primarily invested in teaching us about the form, content, and context of the Bible, I want to turn our attention to our own perspectives and how those perspectives shape our reading. In other words, I want us to think about how the eyes we bring to the Bible cause us to see it in certain ways to the exclusion of others. To keep the optical metaphors in this chapter going, I don't merely want us to try on a different set of glasses; I want us first to try to look at the glasses we are already wearing. This is very difficult to do, but I fear that without a better sense of the history, development, and implications of reading with Cartesian eyes, we may live our entire lives without ever truly loving the Scriptures. I want to wrap up this introduction with a short diagnostic and what I hope will be a helpful illustration of all that we've discussed so far.

Do You Have Cartesian Eyes?

At this point you may already suspect that you've been reading with Cartesian eyes. But let's try to make these abstract ideas more concrete so that we can get a stronger sense of what that means and begin to imagine how it might change. We'll examine Psalm 119:105 as a test case for how we read and what we think it means to understand what we read. How can you tell if you have an instruction-manual view of the Bible? One way to answer this question is to consider what kinds of expectations you bring to the Scriptures. Take a moment to reflect on the questions you ask of the Bible. Perhaps they sound something like these:

What does it mean?
What is the author trying to say?
What is it about?

What is the main idea?

Who is the author?

When was it written?

What does it mean for my life?

If you only ask some versions of these questions, then, like most of us, you probably lean toward an instruction-manual view of the Bible. We tend to focus on ideas and arguments because most of what we read is written to communicate an idea or persuade us of an argument. When I sit down to read an email at work or a book about gardening, I am reading to learn, to become better informed. But what if the kind of training a passage has to offer is not merely intellectual? What if a passage, like Psalm 119:105, is intended to train or correct our hearts?

Remember: the head and the heart are not mutually exclusive. After all, Psalm 119:105 certainly communicates an important idea:

> Your word is a lamp for my feet,
>   a light on my path.

When we read it with Cartesian eyes, we get a simple but important message: we should turn to God's Word when we cannot see where we are going. (Set aside for a moment the fact that the psalmist represents this message using poetic forms such as metaphor, ellipsis, and repetition, rather than simply saying what I said in my paraphrase.) I can understand the main idea of these lines without much work: lamps light up darkness and allow me to see; God's Word is a lamp; if I am in a dark place in life and need to see, I can look to God's Word to light things up and allow me to see where I am or should be going. But if that's all that matters about the verse, then why doesn't the psalmist simply say, "Turn to God's Word for instruction when you don't know what to do"? Writing under the divine inspiration of God, the psalmist could very well have communicated this idea in any number of ways, and yet poetry was the chosen form. The psalmist chose to write a poem, not a proposition. Does that mean there is no claim in the verse? Of course not! Does it mean there's nothing there to instruct our minds? No! What it means is that under-standing the verse requires us to know what makes a poem work and what poems are for.

Psalm 119:105 is not merely trying to teach you information; it is trying to evoke a longing for God's Word in you. If you're a Christian reading the psalm, you probably already know with your head that God's Word should be the default guide for your life. The question is, Is it? Do you treat God's Word this way? When you're in a tough spot, is your first thought, I really just want to read the Bible right now? If the answer is no, then the next question is, Why not? If you *know* that God's Word should be as essential to you as the air you breathe, or light in a dark place, why isn't it? Most likely, it's because you've been taught the Bible is something to be understood with your head, not loved with your heart, or that it is something that can be loved by being understood intellectually. In either case, head is imagined as separate from heart, and perhaps even as more important. If Psalm 119:105 does not evoke longing for God's Word in you, then you do not understand it. Let me say that another way: if you don't feel the longing, then you don't truly understand the verse.

But what would it look like to understand the verse in this way? This is where loving poetry becomes vital. The psalmist uses a meta-phor in Psalm 119:105, calling God's Word a lamp and a light. Of course, God's Word is not a literal light or lamp. You don't flip it on with a switch or ignite it with a match! "Lamp" and "light" are metaphors. Metaphors use familiar, concrete things to make unfa-miliar, abstract things feel more familiar and concrete. You've seen a light; you understand light is helpful in darkness. Great! Your head is in action. But what about your heart? What would it look like to broaden our understanding of the verse to include longing? You will have to allow the metaphor to jump-start your imagination and get your heart running alongside your head.

Try this: You don't know why exactly, but you sit up in bed in the middle of the night. It's very dark. Is it darker than usual? Why can't you see light from the streetlamp outside your window? Did something startle you awake? Did you hear a noise in your sleep? Is that just the refrigerator clicking on in the kitchen? Is it raining? You feel a little flush and your heartbeat is noticeable. You instinctively want to turn on the light. The longing is impulsive, even primal. Light would dispel your fear, make you feel safe, slow your heartbeat. Consider how the psalmist uses light in the metaphor, as something to illuminate his feet and light his path. Have you ever tried to walk down a path in total darkness? I am terrified to walk across my living room with the lights out for fear I might step on a Lego and lose my religion! Nothing will make you long for light like finding yourself in darkness. In such moments, you don't merely know you need light as a logical solution to a problem you're trying to solve. You are drawn to it. You love it. You long for it. The longing is instinctual. Psalm 119:105 is not only trying to persuade you that God's Word is illuminating. It is trying to stir up a longing for God's Word in you. That's part of why the psalmist chose this poetic form rather than just telling you to turn to God's Word. You are supposed to feel a desire, maybe even a desperate desire, for the Scriptures. If you don't feel the desire, it is safe to say that you do not fully understand the verse.

If you don't feel that desire, then, as we have already seen, it may be because you've been trained to read the Bible with Cartesian eyes, to think of it exclusively as an instruction manual. It may sound strange, but if this is the case for you, permit yourself to feel a sense of relief for just a moment. It's okay to feel the same kind of frustration reading Psalm 58 that you felt when a teacher asked you to read T. S. Eliot or Gwendolyn Brooks in school. At least you can now see the problem. You've likely grown up in a culture that values assertions, propositions, and arguments, and there's nothing wrong with those things in themselves. But we cannot be content with this partial understanding and lackluster love. We must cultivate a new hermeneutics and new reading practices that will help us learn to love the Scriptures. We must figure out how to read with our heads *and* our hearts.

Given the head/heart dynamic, a book might seem an odd choice for teaching us to love the Scriptures. After all, aren't books aimed primarily at the head, especially books like this that put forth an argument? That's a fair question. But what I hope will become apparent is that this book, although it is fundamentally an argument, has been crafted with your imagination in mind. As with the meditation on Psalm 119:105 above, I have tried to appeal to the imagination as much as possible in these chapters. I do not set out to change your mind in hopes that your feelings and actions might follow. Instead, I want to foster a kind of intellectual and emotional recognition of how we read the Bible, and I want to work through some practices that can help you become a different reader. It is my hope that if you read this book in good faith and adopt these practices, then, in time, you will look back on how you used to read the Bible and marvel at how much more you've come to love it, and, as a result, love God.

EXERCISE 1
Reflect and Pray for Longing

1. Read Psalm 119:105–12.
2. Write a list of specific things you've longed for or looked forward to recently. For instance,
   a. A visit from family or friends
   b. Publication of a new book by a favorite writer
   c. Release of a new album, movie, television show
   d. A vacation, trip, or event
3. Reflect on what drew you to these things. Why did you look forward to them? How would you describe your longing to a friend?
4. Pray Psalm 119:105 and ask God to give you a longing for his Word more powerful than that for any of these other things.

CHAPTER ONE

How Reading Literature
Became a Quest for Meaning

Perhaps you do not hate poetry. Perhaps you are simply indifferent to it, or maybe you're one of the few who not only enjoy it but also read it regularly. Though I'm primarily writing to those in the first two categories, this book is useful for people in all three, because it explains how we have come to read the way we do and how that mode of reading can be improved. The common reading approach for lovers and haters of poetry alike is to try to interpret the poem. Interpretation is typically understood as solving a puzzle or setting out on a quest for meaning. The difference between the lovers and haters is typically that lovers enjoy the quest and haters do not. Both see the purpose as getting to the climax of the quest, but it's more rewarding for the lovers than the haters. My goal in this chapter is not to convince haters to love the quest. Instead, I want to explain how we came to think about interpretation as a quest for meaning in the first place and how this approach can actually confound our attempts to love the Scriptures.

Most of us do not read only poetry this way. In fact, we tend to read most things as if they contain a meaning we must discover. But poetry seems to present more obstacles to our quest than prose. Informative prose wants to make the meaning clear. The words on the page seem to point directly to ideas. Poetry, on the other hand, seems to obscure its meaning. The words on the page seem to point indirectly to ideas at best. Reading poetry can feel like playing a game with a bunch of complicated and unwritten rules that we didn't ask to play in the first place. When we are guided to the meaning of the poem, our arrival is often presented as an aha moment, a whisking-away of some curtain that was unnecessarily obstructing our view all along, a completion of a quest. We are code breakers trying to decipher an encryption that only a select few with special knowledge are equipped to understand.

As we will see throughout the book, it is this approach we bring to poetry that creates the very frustrations we think of as properties of the poems themselves. Matthew Zapruder argues that "too many of us have been systematically taught to read poetry as if it is full of symbols that stand in for meanings not obviously present in the text itself. The reasons for the pervasiveness of this idea are complex."[1] But what are the reasons? Why do we think of reading poetry as a quest for meaning in the first place? How have we come to think of reading as getting to the point? This chapter offers a brief history of three major influences that have shaped our modern understanding of reading in general and reading poetry in particular. This history will help to answer the questions I've raised here and set us up to consider how our theory of reading (whether conscious or unconscious) shapes, and is shaped by, our attitude and practice.

Imitation

The Greek philosopher Plato developed one of the most influential theories of art in his famous book the *Republic*. The *Republic* is a long dialogue between Plato's teacher Socrates and a handful of

---

1. Matthew Zapruder, *Why Poetry* (New York: Ecco, 2017), 162.

young Athenians who ask Socrates to offer his definition of justice, which he does by casting his vision for an ideal city. Along the way, Socrates makes the seemingly odd claim that he would banish poets from his city. When asked why, he leads his friend Glaucon to the conclusion that poetry, like all other art forms, is fundamentally imitative and thus "far removed from the truth."[2] To understand why Socrates is suspicious of imitation, we must understand a little of his philosophy.

Socrates believes that this world we inhabit is a material embodiment of a more ultimate and immaterial reality. One example he gives to help us wrap our minds around this philosophy is that of a craftsman who builds a bed. Socrates asks Glaucon whether the craftsman makes the *idea* of a bed or if he merely makes *a* bed. Glaucon answers that the craftsman, of course, simply makes *a* bed, not the very *idea* of a bed. The idea of a bed already exists, and the craftsman makes a version of that idea. The idea of the bed must come from a god, Socrates suggests, whereas a bed we can sleep on comes from a craftsman. But then he introduces a painter into the conversation and asks Glaucon what a painter makes when he paints a picture of a bed:

[SOCRATES:] And is a painter also a craftsman and a maker of such things?

[GLAUCON:] Not at all.

[SOCRATES:] Then what do you think he does to a bed?

[GLAUCON:] He imitates it. He is an imitator of what the others make. That, in my view, is the most reasonable thing to call him.

[SOCRATES:] All right. Then wouldn't you call someone whose product is third from the natural one an imitator?

[GLAUCON:] I most certainly would.

[SOCRATES:] Then this will also be true of a [tragic poet], if indeed he is an imitator. He is by nature third from the king and the truth, as are all other imitators.[3]

2. Plato, *Republic* 10.598, 1202.
3. Plato, *Republic* 10.597, 1202.

The poet, like the painter, does not merely imitate the idea of a bed. The poet imitates the appearance of a bed. The problem with art, for Socrates, is that it removes its audience from the truth and asks us to look at an imitation as if it were reality. So what? Well, if we become captivated by an imitation, Socrates argues, we are at risk of abandoning reason and being ruled by fantasy and emotion because an imitation is not bound by reality. It can make of its subject whatever it wishes.

Plato goes on in book 10 of the *Republic* to introduce a dichotomy between poetry and philosophy. And it is this ancient dichotomy that forms the basis of our hermeneutics of information. Poetry is imitative and harmful to the truth, whereas philosophy leads directly to the truth. Poetry stokes passions; philosophy engages reason. Poetry distracts us from reality; philosophy reveals reality to us. Poetry entertains; philosophy instructs.

This dichotomy was new for the Greeks. Prior to Plato and some of his fellow philosophers, poetry was not only considered a source of philosophy and instruction; it was *the* source. "Verse was at that time the mark of excellent discourse, the discourse of authority, no matter its object," argues William Marx.[4] Drama, and especially tragedy, was the most prevalent form of poetry in ancient Athens. According to the philosopher and classicist Martha Nussbaum, in the heyday of Greek poetry, people looked to the poets as their primary sources of ethical instruction: "To attend a tragic drama was not to go to a distraction or a fantasy, in the course of which one suspended one's anxious practical questions. It was, instead, to engage in a communal process of inquiry, reflection, and feeling with respect to important civic and personal ends."[5] Nussbaum goes on to point out how the very environment of an ancient drama contrasts with that of a modern movie theater because it was designed to facilitate civic engagement:

> When we go to the theater, we usually sit in a darkened auditorium, in the illusion of splendid isolation, while the dramatic action . . . is

---

4. William Marx, *The Hatred of Literature*, trans. Nicholas Elliott (Cambridge, MA: Belknap, 2018), 28.

5. Martha Nussbaum, *Love's Knowledge* (New York: Oxford University Press, 1990), 15.

bathed in artificial light as if it were a separate world of fantasy and mystery. The ancient Greek spectator, by contrast, sitting in the common daylight, saw across the staged action the faces of fellow citizens on the other side of the orchestra. And the whole event took place during a solemn civic/religious festival, whose trappings made spectators conscious that the values of the community were being examined and communicated.[6]

No one imagined these plays (which were actually long poems) to be pure entertainment or to be artistic in some sense that set them apart from the practical realities of everyday life. Poetry was both pleasurable and practical, entertaining and instructional.

After Plato, however, the theory of art as imitation cast suspicion on poetry's ability to tell the truth. The result was the emergence of yet another dichotomy, that between form and content. If a writer or speaker wants to tell the truth, why decorate it in frivolous flourishes? Why not just come right out and say it directly? Philosophers like Aristotle who rushed to poetry's defense didn't disagree that poetry was imitative. Rather, they countered that imitative poetry was good and useful. The literary critic Susan Sontag argues that it was such defenses that gave "birth to the odd vision by which something we have learned to call 'form' is separated off from something we have learned to call 'content,' and to the well-intentioned move which makes content essential and form accessory."[7] In other words, from the moment the first defender spoke up to vindicate imitative art, poetry's reputation as imitation was solidified because its value became entangled with the argument for why telling the truth in this imitative form was worthwhile. The case for poetry became a case for why a given content could or should be conveyed in a given form. This separation of form and content engendered the quest for what a text "really says." Sontag makes the bold claim that "all Western consciousness of and reflection upon art have remained within the confines staked out by the Greek theory of art as mimesis [imitation]. . . . None of us can ever retrieve that innocence before all theory when

6. Nussbaum, *Love's Knowledge*, 15–16.
7. Susan Sontag, *Against Interpretation, and Other Essays* (New York: Picador, 2001), 4.

art knew no need to justify itself, when one did not ask of a work of art what it *said* because one knew (or thought one knew) what it *did*."[8] The form of a poem became something we must get through, decipher, move beyond to get to its content. Though the dominant notion of art as imitation has not been toppled in the Western world since Plato (what makes abstract art significant historically is that it's *not* imitative), it has undergone some important transformations. Perhaps the most important of those transformations happened near the end of the eighteenth century, when poetry also came to be viewed as an expression of individual emotion.

Expression

The very notion of poetry, for many of us, may not conjure up the idea of imitation. Instead, poetry may evoke images of romantic figures laying bare their souls. In other words, we may think of poetry primarily in terms of the personal expressions and confessions of an individual. We might envision the poet as a lone and tortured soul with a special artistic gift, someone who is a little weird and who produces these strange little things called poems, which, somehow, occasionally manage to strike a chord in us. After all, what do the subjective musings of an artsy person have to teach us about how to live? But where does this view of poetry as personal expression come from?

Together with his friend Samuel Taylor Coleridge, the British poet William Wordsworth wrote an extremely influential volume of poetry in 1798 entitled *Lyrical Ballads*. When the book was reprinted two years later in 1800, Wordsworth wrote a preface that has become a standard of literary criticism for its articulation of what was then a revolutionary theory of poetry and what has now taken on the power of common sense. While he holds fast to the position that poems are imitative in that they should describe the world, Wordsworth also paradoxically claims that the source of poetry is not in the world itself but in the poet. In the most famous passage from his

8. Sontag, *Against Interpretation*, 4–5.

preface, he argues that "all good poetry is the spontaneous overflow of powerful feelings."[9] The poem is no mere imitation; it is an emanation, something that originates from a source. The source is not the external world, but the poet himself, who is "endued with more lively sensibility, more enthusiasm and tenderness" and "an ability of conjuring up in himself passions."[10] The literary critic M. H. Abrams summarizes the view of poetry as expression this way: "A work of art is essentially the internal made external, resulting from a creative process operating under the impulse of feeling, and embodying the combined product of the poet's perceptions, thoughts, and feelings."[11] The poem is an internal phenomenon rendered external, and the poet is a person specially equipped to do the rendering.

This view of the poem and the poet is different from Plato's. One of the reasons Plato mistrusted the poets is that he believed they were mere conduits, channels, or mouthpieces, who frequently did not understand the words they were reciting because those words originated outside the poets themselves. In contrast, Wordsworth's poet is the source of the poem, and his individuality is, paradoxically, what makes his poems accessible to others. After all, the poet is human, and his job is to take his individual experience and make it representative for all people. As Wordsworth's American friend Ralph Waldo Emerson would exhort, "Doubt not, O poet, but persist. Say 'It is in me, and shall out.' Stand there, balked and dumb, stuttering and stammering, hissed and hooted, stand and strive, until at last rage draw out of thee that *dream*-power which every night shows thee is thine own; a power transcending all limit and privacy, and by virtue of which a man is the conductor of the whole river of electricity."[12] The poet, in Emerson's estimation, is a tenacious prophet learning to channel a surge that flows from within, but he is also "representative. He stands among partial men for the complete man, and apprises us

9. William Wordsworth, "Preface to *Lyrical Ballads*," in *The Critical Tradition: Classic Texts and Contemporary Trends*, ed. David H. Richter (New York: St. Martin's Press, 1989), 287.

10. Wordsworth, "Preface to *Lyrical Ballads*," 290–91.

11. M. H. Abrams, *The Mirror and the Lamp* (Oxford: Oxford University Press, 1971), 22.

12. Ralph Waldo Emerson, "The Poet," in *Selected Essays of Emerson*, ed. Larzer Ziff (New York: Penguin, 2003), 283.

not of his wealth, but of the common wealth."[13] The seeming contradiction is that the poet expresses his internal passions and yet he is also representative. But remember, for Emerson as for Wordsworth, the poet has a special power to render in a way that is accessible to others the sensations and experiences that he has and which "other men are accustomed to feel in themselves."[14]

As with the separation of poetry and philosophy in ancient Athens, Wordsworth's view of poetry as the individual expression of emotion represents a larger cultural change in the Western world at the end of the eighteenth century. Whereas feeling had historically been understood as a public phenomenon, it was now transformed into a private one. In her book *A Revolution of Feeling*, Rachel Hewitt argues that what made Wordsworth's expressive theory so revolutionary was that it located the "origins and expressions of emotion" in the "individual's mind."[15] Prior to the end of the eighteenth century, most writers, historians, and philosophers in Europe conceived of feeling in terms of what they called "the passions." The passions were resolutely public and political; they were a physical, even a biological, capacity; they helped us regulate our responses to external stimuli and manage our relations with others. "Wordsworth displaced emotion from a direct reaction to material circumstances," Hewitt argues. "He described how it is conjured up through memory, not through immediate sensation, and that its purpose is not to instigate moral behavior but to result in an act of imaginative creation, in the form of poetry. Emotion's causes and consequences all begin and end in the individual consciousness."[16] Wordsworth's poetic theory is representative, she insists, of a larger cultural change in which "emotion was approached as an individual rather than collective phenomenon; and the category of 'passions' was replaced by that of 'emotion,' ushering in a depoliticized and frequently negative view of feeling."[17] Unmoored from its prior significance as social, moral,

13. Emerson, "The Poet," 260–61.
14. Wordsworth, "Preface to *Lyrical Ballads*," 291.
15. Rachel Hewitt, *A Revolution of Feeling: The Decade That Forged the Modern Mind* (London: Granta, 2017), 12.
16. Hewitt, *Revolution of Feeling*, 425.
17. Hewitt, *Revolution of Feeling*, 13.

and spiritual regulator, emotion became wholly personal, subjective, and secular.

At the same time that emotion was being transformed from a public to a private phenomenon, poetry was becoming nearly synonymous with the expression of personal emotion. No wonder our default approach to a poem is likely to try to figure out what the author *really* meant to say! We probably think of poetry as the expression of the poet's individual thoughts and emotions, and we think of our job as readers as trying to decipher that expression to get to the thoughts and emotions themselves. Add to that the most influential theories of poetry from the twentieth century, which we'll look at next, and it should be no surprise that most of us struggle with poems. If Plato told us that poems are imitations and Wordsworth said that poems are expressions, then poets and critics in the twentieth century, like T. S. Eliot, taught us that poems can only be understood in relation to a tradition.

Tradition

If you've ever read (or been assigned to read) T. S. Eliot's *The Waste Land*, then it won't be too hard to understand what I mean by poetic tradition. If you've never read the poem, just look it up online, or, even better, find it in a book. It's one of the most anthologized poems in American (and British and "world") literature. Online versions often don't include the many footnotes you'll find in a print version, but even a brief perusal of an online version of the poem will clarify what I mean by tradition. The poem is full of allusions to other poems, stories, plays, writers, and myths. A first-time reader is likely to be overwhelmed when paging/scrolling through the poem. You might wonder, Do I need to read all of the books and poems Eliot references in order to understand his poem?! Though I would not say the poem is impossible to understand without this knowledge of the poetic tradition, I would say that the more you know about the tradition, the more your understanding of the poem will be enhanced. But one consequence of this view of poetry is that it discourages people from reading poetry by making it seem arduous. After all, if an encyclopedic knowledge of literary history is necessary to read a relatively short poem, how many people can truly read it well?

While you have probably been influenced in your thinking about poetry by the theories of imitation and expression, I suspect that this idea of poetry as tradition has affected your view as well, even if it's never been presented to you in this way. What does it mean to view poetry as tradition? In an essay first published in 1919 entitled "Tradition and the Individual Talent," Eliot argued that the emphasis on individuality that dominated poetry for over a century had blinded critics and general readers alike to the fact that the most original parts of the poet's work were often "those in which the dead poets, his ancestors, assert their immortality most vigorously."[18] Tradition, he contended, was not mere impersonation of the previous generation, but a "historical sense" whereby the poet writes "not merely with his own generation in his bones, but with a feeling that the whole of the literature of Europe from Homer and within it the whole of the literature of his own country has a simultaneous existence and composes a simultaneous order. . . . This historical sense . . . is what makes a writer traditional."[19] Poetry is not mere imitation of reality or expression of emotion for Eliot. A poem is a contribution to a timeless conversation that has been going on for millennia and will continue indefinitely.

But how could anyone make such a monumental contribution? Well, for starters the poet must abandon the idea of personal expression. What's important is not the individual personality of the poet but the universal feelings that the poetic tradition expresses. Poets are not the source of poems; they are catalysts. Eliot illustrates his theory with what might seem to us a strange example of a scientific experiment in which a small piece of platinum is put into a chamber containing oxygen and sulfur dioxide: "When the two gases previously mentioned are mixed in the presence of a filament of platinum, they form sulphurous acid. This combination takes place only if the platinum is present; nevertheless the newly formed acid contains no trace of platinum, and the platinum itself is apparently unaffected;

18. T. S. Eliot, "Tradition and the Individual Talent," in *Selected Essays* (New York: Harcourt, Brace, 1950), 4.
19. Eliot, "Tradition and the Individual Talent," 4.

has remained inert, neutral, and unchanged. The mind of the poet is the shred of platinum."[20] The two original gases represent the poetic tradition, or influential works belonging to the tradition. The newly produced sulphurous acid represents the contribution of the poet. The poet is a necessary catalyst in producing the exchange that results in a new product (sulphurous acid). However, notice that the sulphurous acid carries no traces of the platinum; that is, the poet's expression is not an overflow of her own soul. And the platinum is unchanged as well; so the poet is not transformed by the exchange. The result is the creation of something new, though, an addition to the poetic tradition. Poets leverage their knowledge of the tradition, not their personal feelings, to create works of art.

This theory produces a mode of reading that downplays the author and focuses on the poem itself as an autonomous work that must be studied in isolation from the biographical, historical, and social context of the author and reader. In a sense, the poets have been banished once again as they were in Plato's *Republic*! While Eliot's depersonalized poetic tradition may seem fairly technical and far removed from your everyday theory of reading, it has been monumental in its influence. In fact, it has become the dominant theory guiding the way poetry is taught in most English classrooms in secondary and higher education. As Jonathan Culler points out, two of the most popular literature textbooks in the Anglo-American world teach students to think of poems not as expressions of poets but as expressions of a persona or speaker in the poem: "It became a point of doctrine that the speaker of a lyric is to be treated as a *persona*, not as the poet him- or herself, and the focus becomes the drama of attitudes expressed by this speaker-character."[21] Thus many of us were taught in school to read the poem like a puzzle, trying to figure out who the speaker of the poem was and what prompted him or her to speak. If we could figure out those things, perhaps by tracking down any allusions to other literary works in the poetic tradition, then we were on our way to interpreting the poem.

20. Eliot, "Tradition and the Individual Talent," 7.
21. Jonathan Culler, *Theory of the Lyric* (Cambridge, MA: Harvard University Press, 2015), 109.

Implications of Imitation, Expression, and Tradition

Three major consequences of this history are especially relevant to
how we read the Bible, all inseparable from one another. First, we are
likely to take informational writing more seriously than literary writing. Second, we are likely to treat anything we know we're supposed
to take seriously as if it were informational writing. If the truth can be
communicated directly, then a literary telling of the truth will always
be seen as indirect to some extent. While we may praise this indirection
as beautiful, captivating, or meditative, it will always be decoration,
ornamentation, adornment. Whether intentionally or not, we will see
the poetic as frivolous and the informational as serious. When we turn
to a text like the Bible, which we have been told is an instruction manual
for life, it is only natural that we should take it seriously and thus treat
it as informational. The third implication is that most of us don't know
how to read poems because we only know how to read for information.
So if you're wondering why prose writing seems more accessible to you
than poetry, it's at least in part because you probably have an understanding of poetry composed of imitation, expression, and tradition.

While you may not consciously associate reading poetry with any
one of these three theories in particular, they have shaped the way we
think about the nature and purpose of poetry. What all three have in
common is that they encourage us to ask what a poem *really* means.
In other words, if a poem is an imitation of the world, then we are
left trying to get past the words to whatever they *really* represent.
If a poem is an expression of individual emotions, then we read it
with the goal of seeing through the words to whatever the poet must
really have been feeling when they wrote it. And if a poem is a small
piece of a much larger poetic tradition, then we are always reading it to see how it *really* fits into something greater than the poem
itself. In all three cases, the purpose of reading is not to enjoy the
poem itself—though solving the puzzle may bring its own kind of
pleasure—rather, the purpose of reading is to translate the poem, to
convert it into other words. Whatever enjoyment we do experience
comes from getting past or conquering the poem.

The problem with this mode of reading is that converting the
poem into other words to find out what it *really* means is like trying

to understand a painting by erasing, shading, or painting over the existing brush strokes. You're not coming to a better understanding of it; you're changing it into something else. The overall effect of this brief history of ways of thinking about poetry is that we come to see just how synonymous the concepts of *interpretation* and *translation* have become. Sontag puts it like this: "The task of interpretation is virtually one of translation."[22] I don't mean translation in the sense of translating something from one language into another—for example, from English to Spanish. I mean to read something and to put it in other words as a way of understanding it because all that matters is *what is really being said.* When we read poetry, we have been trained (both explicitly and implicitly) to mistrust what's on the page and look for something further, deeper, hidden. If you're wondering why you don't like poetry, or are simply indifferent to it, it's likely because imitation, expression, and tradition have shaped the way you think about the purpose of reading in general and the purpose of reading poetry in particular. Why would you spend time reading poetry, which requires so much work to get to the *real* point, when you could read something that just comes right out and makes the point?

Now that we have a bit of historical background to explain how we came to think of poetry as a quest for content, we are better equipped to pursue the goal of this book: changing our understanding of what it means to read the Bible. The Bible is the greatest poem. By this I mean that it is not merely a message to be interpreted but also an experience to be had. The experience the Bible offers is that of a relationship with God, a communion with our Creator. Shouldn't such a view change your relationship with the text itself? We are called not to complete the quest or conquer the text but to delight in it. Would your joy not change from a conquering satisfaction to a revelatory wonder if you approached the Bible in this way? Culler points out that the pressure to interpret poems is relatively recent:

> In prior centuries readers expected poems to teach and delight; students were not asked to work out the sort of interpretations now deemed proof of serious study. . . . In sum, readers appreciated poems

22. Sontag, *Against Interpretation*, 5.

much as we do songs. We listen to songs without assuming that we should develop interpretations: we take them to illuminate the world, and we sing them to others or to ourselves, point out what we like about them, compare them to other songs by the same and different artists, and generally develop considerable connoisseurship about songs without engaging in interpretation.[23]

None of this is to suggest that we should abandon the Bible as a source of sound doctrine, truth, and instruction. It is to suggest that we expand our understanding of what these things are and how they are communicated so that we might better love the Scriptures and allow them to shape our whole selves, heads and hearts.

Questions for Review

1. Why is Plato critical of art/poetry for being imitative?
2. What is the source of poetry for Wordsworth in his theory of expression?
3. What role does the poet play in producing a poem for T. S. Eliot?
4. What do all three of these concepts—imitation, expression, and tradition—have in common in terms of how they ask readers to think of meaning?

23. Culler, *Theory of the Lyric*, 5.

CHAPTER TWO

The Bible Is Literature

In the introduction I argued that the Bible is not merely an instruction manual designed to inform our heads but also a work of imagination meant to engage our hearts. Then, in chapter 1 I offered some background to explain how reading has become synonymous with a quest for meaning that turns whatever we read into an instruction manual. That theory of reading, or hermeneutics, values getting past the words on the page to whatever meaning they *really* convey. As with reading a step in an instruction manual, the most important thing is always the idea behind the words; the form itself is only important insofar as it communicates the content. But the Bible is more than an instruction manual. It does more than impart information; it seeks to form us as people—intellectually, emotionally, physically, and spiritually. If we don't want to miss that vital spiritual formation, then we need a new hermeneutics, one that is geared toward more than our minds, one that does not focus on getting past the words to the content because it views the Bible as more than an instruction manual.

To develop such a hermeneutics, we must develop our view of the Bible. If it's not only an instruction manual, what else is it? This chapter answers that question by arguing that the Bible is also a work of literature. While this claim is not novel, it does not seem to have much effect on how most Christians read/teach the Bible in their daily lives. The goal of this chapter is twofold: first, to consider what it means to read the Bible as literature; second, to begin outlining a hermeneutics based on this view that will help us read the entire Bible better. This second goal will be carried over into the next few chapters as we work up to an important turn in chapter 5, in which we will rethink the very concept of meaning.

Before you get too worried that we're headed down Wordsworth's path of the romantic artist, let there be no doubt that the Scriptures are intended to instruct us, to improve our minds. "All Scripture is God-breathed and is useful for teaching, rebuking, correcting, and training in righteousness," Paul tells Timothy (2 Tim. 3:16). "Be transformed by the renewing of your mind," he tells the church in Rome (Rom. 12:2). It would seem, then, that we're not mistaken to think of the Bible as an instruction manual. Our goal here is not to dismiss the Bible's power to instruct, but to broaden our understanding of what instruction means. To be instructed is not merely to learn a lesson with your mind and then to allow your mind to guide your actions. Paul exhorts the church at Colossae, "Set your hearts on things above," and, "Set your minds on things above, not earthly things" (Col. 3:1–2). Proverbs 16:23 tells us that "the hearts of the wise make their mouths prudent." The New Testament writers often distinguish between our hearts and our minds. If both heart and mind are important, and if they are different, then they must require different kinds of instruction. To view the Bible as an instruction manual is to approach it exclusively as a book geared toward our minds and to risk missing how it aims to instruct our hearts.

Our purpose in this chapter is to cultivate a view of the Bible that will allow such heart instruction to flourish, and I argue that it is the Bible's literary nature that facilitates such flourishing. But what does it mean to conceive of the Bible as literature? I will focus on two characteristics of works of literature: first, their literariness, or the unique relationship between form and content; second, their appeal to imagination. With this understanding of literature, we'll be ready to move on to reconceptualizing meaning in the following chapters.

Literariness

What is literature? This question has a long history populated by famous philosophers, poets, literary critics, and works of art. But for our purposes, I offer a simple, though admittedly circular, answer: a work of literature is any text that is literary. I know I'm dangerously close to using the word I'm trying to define in my definition! Here's what I mean: for a work to be literary its form must be just as important as, even inseparable from, its content. You'll recall in the last chapter we examined how we came to read literature as a quest for meaning in which we care only about getting to the point, or main idea, of whatever we read. The literary theorist Terry Eagleton argues that to read literature like that is "to go straight for what the poem or novel says, setting aside the way that it says it. To read like this is to set aside the 'literariness' of the work."[1] What makes something a work of literature is its literariness. The question that follows is, What constitutes literariness?

Literariness is made up of all the formal features of a work: its narrative point of view, figurative language, grammar, rhythm, tone, genre, closure, and so on. A work of literature is something for which these features are vital to what is being said. Perhaps it's best to illustrate this idea by contrasting a text for which literariness is not very important with a text for which it is very important. Take as our nonliterary example the "terms of service" on any electronic device or application. What's important about these texts is the information they convey. The words I skim over in English before clicking the obligatory "Accept" button often appear side by side with their counterparts in other languages. So long as the basic information is conveyed, the tone, grammar, and rhythm of the words don't matter very much. Eagleton argues that when we set aside the literariness of a work, we ignore "the fact that it is a poem or play or novel, rather than an account of the incidence of soil erosion in Nebraska."[2] He notes that while we might read the soil report in a "literary" way, by attending to these formal features, this does not necessarily transform it into a work of literature.

1. Terry Eagleton, *How to Read Literature* (New Haven: Yale University Press, 2013), 2.
2. Eagleton, *How to Read Literature*, 2.

In contrast, consider the first line of Anne Bradstreet's poem "The Author to Her Book" as an example of literature. Bradstreet was a seventeenth-century poet who sailed to the Americas with John Winthrop and the Puritans to found the Massachusetts Bay Colony in 1630. She was also responsible for the first book of poems published by a settler, though what we learn from this particular poem is that the volume of her poems was published by a well-intentioned family member without her knowledge or permission. After discovering that her book had been exposed to the public, she wrote "The Author to Her Book" as something of a defense of her work. The first line reads: "Thou ill-formed offspring of my feeble brain," and the literariness of its composition is integral. Unlike the "terms of service" agreement on your phone, this poem will no longer be the same poem if you change one word of this line. Here's the entire poem:

> Thou ill-formed offspring of my feeble brain,
> Who after birth didst by my side remain,
> Till snatched from thence by friends, less wise than true,
> Who thee abroad, exposed to public view,
> Made thee in rags, halting to th' press to trudge,   5
> Where errors were not lessened (all may judge).
> At thy return my blushing was not small,
> My rambling brat (in print) should mother call,
> I cast thee by as one unfit for light,
> The visage was so irksome in my sight;   10
> Yet being mine own, at length affection would
> Thy blemishes amend, if so I could.
> I washed thy face, but more defects I saw,
> And rubbing off a spot still made a flaw.
> I stretched thy joints to make thee even feet,   15
> Yet still thou run'st more hobbling than is meet;
> In better dress to trim thee was my mind,
> But nought save homespun cloth i' th' house I find.
> In this array 'mongst vulgars may'st thou roam.
> In critic's hands beware thou dost not come,   20
> And take thy way where yet thou art not known;

> If for thy father asked, say thou hadst none;
> And for thy mother, she alas is poor,
> Which caused her thus to send thee out of door.[3]

Every word has been arranged in relation to every other word to produce a specific tone, mood, pace, and rhythm. The grammar, syntax, and word order are precariously balanced. Most importantly, these formal arrangements contribute to the meaning of the lines. This may seem like overkill. Returning to the first line, why couldn't you exchange a word like "offspring" and still get the same effect? For one reason, to change that word could throw off the rhythm of the line. What if you were to substitute a word like *child*, *babe*, or *progeny*? These words don't have the same number of syllables as *offspring*, and the line needs ten syllables for the rhythm to work. Did you notice that every line has ten syllables? This poem is written in a verse form called iambic pentameter, where each line is composed of five feet, and each foot is made up of two syllables, one unstressed and one stressed. Each foot is called an "iamb," and there are *five* feet in each line, so it's called iambic *penta*meter. To read the line with the right rhythm looks like this:

Thou ILL-formed OFFspring OF my FEEble BRAIN,

You can read the line correctly by emphasizing the syllables that appear in capitals. I might represent it rhythmically like this:

duh-DUH duh-DUH duh-DUH duh-DUH duh-DUH

But why is the rhythm so important? There are many reasons. First, the verse form that produces this rhythm (iambic pentameter) was made popular in the English language by Geoffrey Chaucer a couple centuries before Bradstreet was born and used famously by William Shakespeare just before Bradstreet came of age. By writing in this meter Bradstreet is using a form that will be familiar to her

---

3. Anne Bradstreet, "The Author to Her Book," Poetry Foundation, accessed March 12, 2020, https://www.poetryfoundation.org/poems/43697/the-author-to-her-book.

audience. Second, the rhythm itself mimics a rocking motion like that you might use to soothe a baby, creating a physical consonance between the feel of the poem and its central metaphor of a small child. Third, if she had not used some kind of regular meter, then these two lines would lose some of their power:

> I stretched thy joints to make thee even feet,
> Yet still thou run'st more hobbling than is meet;

Notice how these lines depend on the reader's knowledge of poetic feet, in this case iambs, for the metaphor to work on multiple levels. A child with malformed feet may hobble, and a poem with uneven feet will not move evenly like a smooth line of iambic pentameter should. If the poem did not utilize a regular meter, we would be left wondering why she's talking about the poor child's feet.

But you may object, couldn't we replace "offspring" with a similar word that also has two syllables? Maybe *baby*, *infant*, or *newborn*? Well, no, I don't think so for three main reasons. First, and most practically, we don't know for sure that the "offspring" is so young. Second, there aren't that many good two-syllable words in English for "child" that don't sound awkward in the line. "Thou ill-formed *youngster* of my feeble brain" just doesn't have the same ring to it. Third, the word "offspring" refers not only to children but also to anything "which springs from or is produced by something," according to the *Oxford English Dictionary*. The word thus works on both the literal and the figurative levels Bradstreet invokes.

The vitality of this single word illustrates the literariness of "The Author to Her Book." We could spend a long time examining every formal aspect of the poem, all the while deepening our understanding of it, because the language, rhythm, and arrangement are essential to the meaning. Or, another way of saying it is that the *way* the poem speaks is inseparable from *what* it says. If we were to replace the word "offspring," the poem would no longer mean the same. Works of literature *are* what they say, whereas nonliterary works *mean* what they say.

But what does it mean to say that the work *is* what it *says*? In an essay on the fiction of James Joyce, playwright Samuel Beckett claims that Joyce's "writing is not about something; it is that something itself."[4] The work of literature should not be read for what it points to but for what it is. Though I don't want to get ahead of myself here, the implications for reading the Bible should jump out at us immediately. The Scriptures do not merely point to God; they are God-breathed (2 Tim. 3:16). We are told time and again that the Scripture is God's Word, that we are to hear the Word of the Lord. And then in the prologue to John's Gospel, we are told that Jesus himself is the Word (John 1:1). Of course, the Bible points us to him, but it is also his very revelation!

We hold his revelation in our hands but treat the form as an inconsequential impediment to the content when that is the very thing in which we should be delighting. When we separate form from content, we are left with something that is less than God's Word, most importantly, but also with something in which it is difficult to delight. If the literariness of the Bible was not important, then it wouldn't be there at all, let alone play such an important role. In an influential essay entitled "The Heresy of Paraphrase," the twentieth-century literary scholar Cleanth Brooks argues that the more we talk *about* a poem, the further away we get from understanding it. He claims that one of the biggest problems with understanding poetry is that we "take certain remarks which we make *about* the poem—statements about what it says or about what truth it gives or about what formulations it illustrates—for the essential core of the poem itself."[5] Brooks's point reminds me of a sermon I once heard on Psalm 117 in which the preacher referenced Martin Luther's commentary on that psalm. He noted the humor in the fact that while the psalm was only two short verses, Luther's commentary on it runs to nearly forty pages! Later, I borrowed the volume of Luther's commentaries that included Psalm 117 from a friend and confirmed the story, chuckling to myself thinking that it almost seemed that the more Luther wrote about the psalm, the further away he got from what makes it important.[6]

4. Samuel Beckett, "Dante . . . Bruno . . . Vico . . . Joyce," in *Disjecta: Miscellaneous Writings and a Dramatic Fragment; Samuel Beckett*, ed. Ruby Cohn (New York: Grove Press, 1984), 27.
5. Cleanth Brooks, "The Heresy of Paraphrase," in *The Well Wrought Urn* (New York: Harcourt, Brace, 1975), 199.
6. Martin Luther, "Psalm 117," trans. Edward Sittler, in *Luther's Works*, vol. 14, *Selected Psalms III*, ed. Jaroslav Pelikan (St. Louis: Concordia, 1958), 1–39.

What was Luther's mistake? Brooks would call it "the heresy of paraphrase." What he means is that, in our efforts to explain the literary work, we mistake our explanation for the thing itself. In other words, we read the psalm, and then we spend forty pages explaining what it means. Ultimately, we come to commit a literary heresy because we begin to appeal not to the work itself but to our interpretation of it as authoritative. Nothing in Luther's forty pages on Psalm 117 *is* the meaning of the psalm. Only the psalm itself *is* its meaning. A listener once asked the great composer Robert Schumann to explain an especially difficult musical piece. Instead of speaking, Schumann sat down and played the piece again.[7] Brooks insists that the "prose-sense," or what I might call the main idea, "of the poem is not a rack on which the stuff of the poem is hung."[8] In other words, the form of the composition is not mere decoration for the content. Schumann cannot explain the piece in other words. If someone asks, "What does Psalm 117 mean?" the best answer is to read Psalm 117, because of its literariness.

Imagination

The tragedy for most modern readers is that we have not been taught to tune in to the literariness of what we read. This is especially true when it comes to reading the Bible, and the result is, as we saw in the last chapter, that we come to focus exclusively on the main idea, or message, of the Scriptures. As Leland Ryken notes, "Traditional approaches to the Bible lean heavily toward the conceptual and doctrinal. This is largely the result of the modern assumption that a person's world view and conception of truth are intellectual or ideational only."[9] This conception plays out in our preference for the heresy of paraphrase over the actual texts themselves. We have been trained to go after what the text *says* so that we can think differently, retrain our minds, get our heads on straight. But works of literature

7. George Steiner, *Real Presences* (Chicago: University of Chicago Press, 1989), 20.
8. Brooks, "Heresy of Paraphrase," 199.
9. Leland Ryken, *Words of Delight: A Literary Introduction to the Bible* (Grand Rapids: Baker, 1992), 15.

do more (not less!) than change the way we think. They capture our imaginations.

Literary texts don't merely explain information; they give us images, visions, worlds to help us imagine. Ryken has written perhaps more than any other contemporary literary critic about the literariness of the Bible. He argues that "literature appeals to our understanding through our imagination." What does this mean for reading the Bible? Ryken answers: "The Bible gives us pictures of life and reality as well as ideas. Its truth sometimes consists of ideas and propositions, but in its literary parts truth often takes the form of *truthfulness to reality in human experience.*"[10] When we read works of literature, our approach should be different than when we read nonliterary works or works that only occasionally exhibit literariness. We should be reading for the experiences of recognition, shock, delight, enchantment, even entertainment. There is a kind of instruction we can receive from the Bible that cannot be rearticulated as a proposition or series of factual statements. But what kind of instruction is this?

Ryken helps us understand how literary writing instructs in his analysis of Genesis 4. Genesis 4 tells the story of how Cain murders his brother Abel, but the writing aims to do more than inform us of the facts of the matter. To understand the story, readers must also get a sense of the tragedy. They must be moved by the story: "If we *recognize* and *feel* the horror of Cain's behavior in the story of Cain and Abel, we have grasped the truth of the story."[11] The implication is that if we do *not* recognize and feel the horror, then we have not grasped the truth of the story. If you come to the story solely as a work of history or information and not as a work of literature, you will focus only on what lessons might be learned from the story, how the story fits into the time line of Genesis, or what it can tell us about the doctrine of sin. All these things are important and worthy of our attention. But the story also wants us to *feel* the tragedy. After all, Cain knew it was wrong to murder his brother, and many people who have committed similar sins have known the story of Cain and

10. Ryken, *Words of Delight*, 15.
11. Ryken, *Words of Delight*, 15.

Abel. Genesis 4 is about more than teaching us the difference between right and wrong; it is invested in laying the weight of horror on our shoulders. It wants to render the dreadfulness and the shock of sin so real to us that we are repulsed by the violence. When we miss the dread and shock, we misread, or at least underread, Genesis 4.

Imaginative writing also differs from informational writing in how it asks and answers questions. More often than not, informational writing sets out to answer a question as definitely as it can, or at least to consider what the possible answers are, or perhaps to clarify the question itself. In contrast, literary texts, and especially poems, are less concerned with certainty than with rumination and reflection. As Zapruder suggests, "Maybe poems are not to be read for their great answers, but for their great, more often than not unanswerable, questions."[12] Zapruder does not mean to suggest that poems can be about whatever we want, or that they have no answers and thus no meaning. He is merely making sense of an observation he's made about poems. Oftentimes, they are contradictory and paradoxical in ways that propositional prose writing is not, and so perhaps they are supposed to be that way.

I do not mean to suggest that when we encounter a question that goes unanswered in a work of literature, we should somehow give up on it and imagine it as unanswerable. May it never be! I am arguing, rather, that the purpose of addressing such a problem in a work of literature may be different than the purpose of addressing it in a work of informational prose. In a biblical context, Paul might have very specific things to say about how to address people who are behaving foolishly in the church. Perhaps he does not address the specifics of the situation your local congregation is facing, and so you could say that the Bible doesn't speak directly to your particular challenge. But you can draw general principles from his specific instructions to make your decisions. In contrast, what do we do with a contradiction like the one found in Proverbs 26:4–5?

> Do not answer a fool according to his folly,
> or you yourself will be just like him.

12. Matthew Zapruder, *Why Poetry* (New York: Ecco, 2017), 107.

> Answer a fool according to his folly,
> or he will be wise in his own eyes.

If we were to read this passage the same way we read a passage from one of Paul's Epistles, we might conclude that the text is somehow inaccurate or flawed or untrue. But such struggle is natural to literary texts, which encourage us to reflect and meditate rather than to cut to the chase. Zapruder encourages us along these lines: "Instead of objecting to, or trying to reconcile with a single overarching interpretation, the contradictions or lack of an overall coherence of thought in a poem, it is best to embrace that strangeness, to think about what questions it raises, and to let those questions lead us to the deeper thinking the poem exists to produce."[13] The purpose of a literary text is to activate our imaginations, to encourage us to pause, to wrestle, to reflect. The writer of Proverbs did not have to create this contradiction, but did! Why? Isn't it a bit confusing? Only if your goal in reading it is to get past the poetry to what the poem *says*. Doesn't it give us pause, cause us to remark, "What?!" Of course, but that's exactly what we're supposed to do. Literary texts are not always designed to get to the point. They are often designed to get us to ponder.

So What?

As you have no doubt experienced, everyday life is filled with confusing joys and messes. The Bible doesn't always have a direct answer tailored to every possible situation. Think of any number of public, personal, political, ecclesial challenges you've encountered in your own life. How many times have you wished that the Bible spoke to your specific circumstance? Of course, we have basic instructions and guiding principles that we know are true, but it's not always immediately clear how they are to be enacted in every situation. Such moments of uncertainty and ambiguity call for the kind of deep consideration that literary texts cultivate in us. Rather than looking for *the* answer in the Bible and twisting passages to fit your needs,

13. Zapruder, *Why Poetry*, 109.

why not turn to the more literary parts that withhold answers in favor of encouraging reflection on the paradoxical, even ineffable, aspects of life? Should I answer the fool or not? Maybe you need to meditate on those verses from Proverbs and see where God leads you in this specific circumstance.

At this point, I hope it's clear that I am not arguing for two different kinds of writing in the Bible, the literary and the instructional. Instead, I am insisting that the whole of God's Word is useful for instruction (among other things) and that this instruction takes different forms, one of which is literary. When we treat the whole of the Scriptures as if all their instruction were the same, we risk missing out on the multifaceted nature of God's instruction and thus hazard neglecting obedience to him and, just as bad, forgoing communion with him. Sometimes, a text instructs us not by telling us exactly what to think or do but by prompting us to reflect on a problem, idea, emotion, or person. Paul might tell us in 1 Corinthians 13 that love is patient, whereas the story of Hosea and Gomer causes us to marvel at the patience required to love a spouse who is so defiantly unfaithful. And, of course, in that marveling we are led to reflect on God's patience with his people.

Literary texts thus *mean* in different ways than nonliterary texts. That is, they are equally meaningful, but they *mean* differently. They signify in a different way than propositional writings. To understand a work of literature is different from understanding a nonliterary work. Remember that the purpose of this book is not to tell you important historical, cultural, political, and linguistic information about the biblical texts themselves. Biblical scholars can help you understand those things. Rather, I want to help us (1) to pay attention to the way we approach the Bible and (2) to develop a more sophisticated, robust, and fitting approach to reading. The other major purpose is (3) to revise our concept of the Bible itself as a text. It is so much more than a how-to manual. It is meaningful in ways that we can't quite articulate and in ways that are not immediately useful in a practical sense. It does not always seek to communicate a neat and tidy message, and yet the most ineffable passages are deeply meaningful. And yet, if meaning is not merely the message or central idea of the text, then what is meaning? If understanding isn't only going in search of the meaning and finding it, then what is understanding? The next chapter takes up these questions and argues that meaning itself is more than a message, that understanding is more than an intellectual activity.

EXERCISE 2
Reading with Imagination

1. Read Genesis 4.
2. Write a list of literary features in the chapter. The purpose is to attend to how the passage is appealing to your imagination.
   a. Details about characters
   b. Emphases on conflict
   c. Appeals to imagination
3. Reflect on how you would describe the scene the passage asks you to imagine. What emotions does the scene produce?
4. Pray that God would bring his words to life in your reading of the Scriptures.

CHAPTER THREE

Meaning Is More
Than Message

What is meaning? For most of us, our default concept of the meaning of a text is likely to be something like the main idea in the text, the central concept, or the point. But if you go looking for the main idea in a text that is not trying to give you one, you're going to be very frustrated. Since literature is often interested in what is ineffable, when you're reading a literary text, you're going to run into passages that do not have a singular main idea. The argument of this chapter is that we need a more robust concept of meaning if we are to learn to love the Scriptures well. If the Bible is filled with works of literature and if those literary texts are aimed at our imaginations, then it follows that to ask what they mean is different from asking what nonliterary, or less literary, texts mean. Another way of putting this is to say that understanding a work of literature is different from understanding a work whose literariness is less important. We need much bigger notions of both meaning and understanding.

At the close of the previous chapter, I claimed that works of literature *mean* differently than nonliterary works. I'm using the word *mean* here as a verb; I'm arguing that literature signifies, communicates, connects with us differently than nonliterature. If nonliterary texts most often mean by *telling* us what we're supposed to understand as directly as possible, literary texts mean by creating a world in which we must imagine ourselves. Only when we've acclimated ourselves to the world of the text and made sense of how things work there will we begin to understand what it means. Right from the beginning, then, it should be clear that when we talk about what a work means, not only could the answer be different for many different texts but so also could the *ways we answer* be very different for many different *kinds* of texts.

My goal in this chapter is complicated because that default concept of meaning is so strong. On the one hand, it might be best simply to stop asking what works of literature mean as a way of discouraging us from reducing them to some central idea! But that is a bit of an overcorrection, as literature (and, of course, the Bible) is deeply meaningful. So we must take the much harder route of remaking our default concept of meaning. I will admit right up front that such a change in perspective cannot be accomplished by reading a single chapter in a book, though I hope this will make a good start. You will have to take this chapter to heart and carry the examples I offer here beyond the pages of this book into your own reading life.

From the beginning, you'll have to ask yourself, Do I want to understand the Bible? This might seem like a disingenuous question, but it's a question we should all seriously ask ourselves. After all, if you come to understand the Bible better, consider the implications for how you live, think, and speak. Understanding the Bible better may very well unsettle you; it may estrange you from yourself as you try to grow into someone who loves the Scriptures better. If this line of thought seems abstract, think of it like this: Have you ever shared a favorite song, movie, or GIF with a friend, only to have them not be quite as enthusiastic about it as you are? What's your first thought? If you're like me, you're inclined to think concerning your friend, She doesn't really *get* it. Why do I have that thought? Well, because I have been so affected by the thing that the only imaginable response is the kind of enthusiasm *I* experienced. If my friend *really* understood, she would feel the same way, right? If you come to understand the Bible better, you will be the kind of person who is moved by it and who wants others to be moved as well. Is that something you truly want? If so, then we must rethink how texts mean and how readers understand.

Meaning as Emotion, Understanding as Feeling

Literary texts are more interested in emotional meaning than nonliterary texts. To understand literature, then, you must experience the feelings it sets out to evoke. While both literary and nonliterary texts instruct us, because literary texts appeal primarily to our imaginations they typically evoke emotions differently than nonliterary texts. While a political speech or fiery sermon may appeal to our emotions, their purpose in doing so is usually to persuade us, to move us in the direction of their main point, argument, or idea. With literature, emotion itself is often the point. This is especially true of poetry. The literary critic Helen Vendler argues that "the primary aim of a lyric is not to state an idea but to enact an emotion."[1] Thus, if you do not feel an emotion when you read a poem, the primary aim of the passage is lost on you.

While we may have been taught to separate emotion from meaning, there is a kind of emotional meaning that is vital to understanding literature and the world. The poet Muriel Rukeyser calls this "emotional truth" and claims that what makes a poem special is that it "invites you to feel. More than that: it invites you to respond." She continues: "This response is total, but it is reached through the emotions. A fine poem will seize your imagination intellectually—that is, when you reach it, you will reach it intellectually too—but the way is through emotion, through what we call feeling."[2] Poems activate your intellect through your emotion. But to experience this emotional activation, you must engage in the kind of "total response" Rukeyser describes. What does this mean? What does she mean when she says poems demand a total response? What would a less-than-total response look like?

1. Helen Vendler, "Author's Notes for Teaching *Poems, Poets, Poetry*," in *Poems, Poets, Poetry: An Introduction and Anthology*, ed. Helen Vendler, 3rd ed. (New York: St. Martin's Press, 2010), 4.
2. Muriel Rukeyser, *The Life of Poetry* (Ashfield, MA: Paris Press, 1996), 11.

If I were to make a case that Saint Augustine significantly influenced Saint Thomas Aquinas, you would not need to immerse yourself in the argument to understand the assertion, its supporting reasons, and the accompanying evidence. That is, you do not need to be invested with your whole being to comprehend the claim. You do not need to enter the world of either figure, or my world either, to understand what's at issue. If I make the case forcefully and provide enough reasons and evidence, then my position will be clear. But literature doesn't work like that. To understand a poem, you must engage it with your whole self: heart, soul, mind, and strength. You must accept the premises of the world the poem is creating, acquiesce to that world, commit yourself to its realities, and play by its rules. Oftentimes, I ask my students to close their eyes and imagine something. Only those who are willing to go along with the game will be able to comprehend the exercise. You must play the game to understand.

Have you ever been an unwilling participant in a children's game? If you have children, watch children, work with children, or interact with them at all, you will know the feeling of playing halfheartedly with children who are wholly committed to whatever they are playing. You don't experience the same joy and fun of the game, because you are not fully committed. If you could just give in to the ridiculousness of the game, you would enjoy it differently, but it's hard for self-aware adults to play without worrying about what others will think. At the risk of associating poetry with childishness, that's the kind of "total response" Rukeyser has in mind. To understand a poem, or any work of literature, you must be willing to give yourself to the world of the text. You must be willing to play the game of the literary world like a child plays.

That sounds very nice, but what does it look like practically? How can we begin to respond totally, to connect with a work of literature on such an emotional level? Let's consider an example from a poem I love. One moment of emotional connection can open a door to the entire poem. Robert Frost was an American poet who was born in the 1870s and lived to read at John F. Kennedy's inauguration. He remains one of the most well-known and beloved poets in American history. One of his early poems, "Birches," offers what is, for me, an opportunity for the kind of commitment to the world of the text that I've been discussing. "Birches" is written in the voice of a grown man meditating on what he thinks about when he sees birch trees. In case you've never seen a birch tree, I'll mention here that they have papery bark and are very flexible. Frost's poem imagines them bending under the weight of ice in winter; it imagines a young boy climbing them until they bend down and the boy leaps back to the ground. It's this second image that offers an entrance to the world of the poem for me every time I read it, because the tension and suspense that builds up just before the boy leaps is compared so vividly to the act of overfilling a cup:

> . . . He always kept his poise
> To the top branches, climbing carefully
> With the same pains you use to fill a cup
> Up to the brim, and even above the brim.
> Then he flung outward, feet first, with a swish,
> Kicking his way down through the air to the ground.[3]

". . . and even above the brim." It's that image of the cup that gets me every time. We've likely all had this experience of overfilling a cup but stopping before the water, tea, or coffee runs down the side. The liquid appears to be higher than the brim of the cup. How is this possible? The poet, too, has experienced this, and now he is using that experience and the awe of impossibility that goes along with it to invite us into the emotional truth of the poem. That sense of careful wonder is the same sense of the boy who climbs the birches. If we will begin to play the game of the poem, such connections multiply exponentially, even if we can't quite imagine climbing trees like this.

There are two levels of feeling at work here. First, there is the feeling of recognition, of recognizing in the poem either yourself or something you've done. We have all tried to fill a cup so full that it won't hold one more drop but not so full that it overflows and, in so doing, have witnessed the seemingly impossible spectacle of a cup filled above the brim. This kind of recognition is what makes the humor of an observational comic like Jerry Seinfeld so funny. He makes jokes about things that are so mundane they don't seem to

3. Robert Frost, "Birches," Poets.org, Academy of American Poets, accessed February 17, 2020, https://poets.org/poem/birches.

be worth our attention, but he's wildly successful because they are things we all experience. So when someone else takes notice of the stingy faucets in airport bathrooms, how to respond to telemarketers, or the mystery of how one would plant a seedless watermelon, we laugh because we've had these very thoughts. Second, there is the feeling generated by the actual image. In this case, it's that sense of carefulness you feel when pouring and the sense of tension you feel as the liquid approaches the brim. Finally, it's the sense of wonder at the fullness. Can you access those feelings? I don't mean, Can you remember them? I mean, Can you conjure them? Can you feel them, now, as you read the poem? The young boy climbs the birch tree with that same carefulness and tension. He experiences the same wonder as the tree begins to bend and he flings himself outward to the ground. If you can commit to the world of the poem, you can feel the actual emotions yourself. When you feel them, you are understanding the poem. Let me say that another way: that feeling is (part of) what the poem means. To understand is to feel; to feel is to understand.

The implication of this argument that "to understand is to feel" is that if you do not feel you do not understand. While this is not equally true of all kinds of texts, it is almost always true of literary texts. Literature is, in fact, one of the realms in which, as the philosopher Martha Nussbaum contends, "the pursuit of intellectual reasoning apart from emotion will actually prevent a full rational judgment."[4] We need emotion to understand literature. Thus, to ask what a literary text means is always to ask what kinds of emotions it evokes. But my main point here is that to understand literature we must do more than identify or acknowledge these emotions. We must feel them.

Meaning as Defamiliarization, Understanding as Reseeing

Works of literature also activate our understanding by making the familiar and normal seem unfamiliar and strange. In other words, sometimes what a text means is the way it makes you see your world

4. Martha C. Nussbaum, *Love's Knowledge: Essays on Philosophy and Literature* (New York: Oxford University Press, 1990), 41.

in a new way. As we live our lives and have the same experiences over and over again, we become habituated and desensitized to things that are, in reality, wondrous, terrible, beautiful, and awesome. Consider the many firsts you have experienced in your life: your first step, your first day in school, your first bike, your first drive, your first kiss, your first job, your first child, your first day of retirement. Even the most novel and exciting first can become, over time, a mundane part of our existence. I remember wanting my driver's license so badly for so long, and while I'm sure there are some who never lose the zest for driving, for most of us in regions and cultures where driving is routine, the act of getting behind the wheel loses its newness over time. Even the explosive joy of your first child, an unfathomable miracle, can wear off as you settle into the regimen necessary to keep your baby and yourself alive and well. When we become numb to such experiences, we tend to lose sight of just how amazing life can be. It's as if we lose a kind of understanding we once had.

It's true that we can simply tell ourselves that the beautiful and terrible things we become accustomed to are, well, beautiful and terrible, but literature sets out to renew our understanding by making those things which have become familiar unfamiliar once again. Art thus creates a special kind of understanding in which we are able to resee things we've lost sight of; it encourages a kind of reunderstanding. The Russian literary critic and theorist Viktor Shklovsky argues that "art exists that one may recover the sensation of life; it exists to make one feel things, to make the stone *stony*."[5] What could be more mundane than the stoniness of a stone? And yet a good painting or poem can evoke a new sight or feeling of a thing as everyday as a rock. Shklovsky continues: "The technique of art is to make objects 'unfamiliar,' to make forms difficult, to increase the difficulty and length of perception because the process of perception is an aesthetic end in itself and must be prolonged."[6] Many poems are short, and yet they can take just as long to read as a longer piece of prose. Why? They are arranged in ways that prevent us from settling into our

5. Viktor Shklovsky, "Art as Technique," in *The Critical Tradition: Classic Texts and Contemporary Trends*, ed. David H. Richter (New York: St. Martin's Press, 1989), 741.
6. Shklovsky, "Art as Technique," 741.

comfortable, default perspectives. Shklovsky insists that "art removes objects from the automatism of perception."[7] When we don't have recourse to our automatic ways of understanding, we must see even the most familiar things in new ways. Poets and critics have long called this phenomenon "defamiliarization."

Claude McKay's poem "Subway Wind" defamiliarizes the New York City subway in a way that grips me every time I read it. McKay was a native of Jamaica who immigrated to the United States in 1912 and found himself at the forefront of a literary revolution in the 1920s now known as the Harlem Renaissance. His poems engage everything from island life to lynching, and he never flinches in the face of the beautiful or the violent. I want to look at a simple example of defamiliarization in the opening lines of "Subway Wind" in hopes that it will be easy to grasp and thus easy to recognize and experience in other poems. The poem begins with these lines:

> Far down, down through the city's great, gaunt gut
> The gray train rushing bears the weary wind;
> In the packed cars the fans the crowd's breath cut,
> Leaving the sick and heavy air behind.[8]

The title signals the subject of the poem, and so we know the "weary wind" in the second line is the "Subway Wind" of the title. The first line always grabs me: "Far down, down through the city's great, gaunt gut." I'm not from a big city, but I've ridden enough subways to know what it's like to stand on a platform in an underground tunnel waiting for a train to come rumbling out of the darkness. I imagine folks who ride the subway every day no longer think much about their surroundings. They become so acclimated to the subterranean world that they forget they are hurtling through caves. McKay makes the familiar tunnels strange by imagining them as the "gut" of the city. He turns the city into a person and the subway tunnels into the person's guts. When you stand on the platform waiting for the train, you're standing in the city's intestines! I know it's kind of gross, but

7. Shklovsky, "Art as Technique," 742.
8. Claude McKay, *Harlem Shadows: The Poems of Claude McKay* (New York: Harcourt, Brace, 1922), 54.

that's the point. Imagine the air trapped in your guts. The relief of getting on the train is "Leaving the sick and heavy air behind." Next time you're waiting for a subway train, imagine yourself standing in the intestines of New York, Rio de Janeiro, London, Addis Ababa, or Tokyo. The poem prevents us from merely picturing a subway tunnel. We find ourselves thinking longer and harder about a fairly mundane action. Don't worry about the "point" or "idea" of this defamiliarization. The very experience itself is meaningful.

The meaning of the defamiliarization is this heightened experience of the everyday. To put the notions of "understanding as feeling" and "understanding as reseeing" together, we might say that to feel this strange relation to an otherwise familiar object or experience *is* to understand what's happening in the poem. The defamiliarization is the meaning. Vendler argues that the purpose of a lyric poem is to put "a new spin on an old emotion. We call this new spin 'imagination.' To imagine the world freshly is the task of the world's artists."[9] There are no new emotions, as the writer of Ecclesiastes told us so long ago:

> What has been will be again,
>   what has been done will be done again;
>   there is nothing new under the sun.
> Is there anything of which one can say,
>   "Look! This is something new"?
> It was here already, long ago;
>   it was here before our time. (Eccles. 1:9–10)

The artist doesn't invent anything new. She helps us to see the same old things in new ways. This new kind of seeing is, itself, a form of understanding. Thus, the "new spin on an old emotion" or the re-imagining of something familiar is, itself, a form of meaning.

Part of what it means to understand the meaning of a verse like Psalm 119:105 is to reimagine what God's Word is via the experience of being surprised by the writer's metaphorical rendering of it as a lamp. A word is not a lamp, after all. So what does the verse mean?

9. Vendler, "Author's Notes," 5.

Well, if we're asking that question in the conventional sense of, What is the main idea? it should be evident by now that the question is a bit silly. The verse is designed not to state an idea but to enact an emotion, to defamiliarize God's Word and help us see it anew and engage it differently. I do not mean to suggest that there are no ideas wrapped up in this experience. Of course there are, but the primary meaning of the verse is this newness, this fresh relation to the Word. To be perplexed, surprised, caught off guard by the image of God's Word as a lamp is to understand the verse. This sense of meaning is much richer than the simplistic notion of a main idea. It does not reduce the text to a propositional statement nor readers to "brains-on-a-stick," as James K. A. Smith likes to say.[10]

Meaning as Association, Understanding as Making Peace

The first two theories of meaning in this chapter should help prepare us for this third and final idea of meaning as association. This may sound, by turns, vague or technical, but think of it like this: sometimes a text means by making you think of other things. There is great value in recognizing the connections between things, though this kind of association may feel unsatisfying since we've been so thoroughly trained to look for a singular main idea. If meaning is, in part, associative, then it is not always clear-cut, singular, or even articulable. Thus, to understand a text sometimes means to make peace with the fact that it cannot be boiled down to a neat and tidy message.

Literary texts tend to open things up rather than tying them up. In his book *Why Poetry*, Zapruder recalls how he once received a letter from a woman who described reading poetry as a "drifting experience." For the woman, this drifting was the source of much frustration as it made her feel as if she never quite arrived at a place where she could "get" poetry. But Zapruder is encouraged by this feeling of drift: "This drifting feeling she describes so well is what a reader can experience, and might have an instinct to resist. When we release ourselves from the need to boil the poem down to a single meaning or theme, the mind can move

10. James K. A. Smith, *You Are What You Love: The Spiritual Power of Habit* (Grand Rapids: Brazos, 2016), 3.

in a dreamlike, associative way. This associative movement in poetry can at first feel disorienting, but it is actually quite close to the way parts of our minds, unbeknownst to our conscious selves, constantly function, simultaneously attentive to the outside world, but also thinking, processing, half dreaming."[11] That drifting association is an important way in which poems mean. Zapruder explains that this is what initially frustrated him about the poet John Ashbery. Ashbery's poems seemed to refuse neat and tidy conclusions. But over time Zapruder realized that this resistance to a singular idea is integral to how a poem works: "Just when it seems as if it is going to collect into a larger point, a unifying idea, it refuses to. Some people read poems, feel this way, and think they do not know enough about poetry; others resent poetry for not behaving like other forms of writing."[12] I would argue that these feelings of inadequacy and resentment stem from our limited concept of understanding. If we no longer associate understanding exclusively with our ability to locate and summarize a main idea, then we will shed these feelings of inadequacy and resentment when reading literature in general and poetry in particular.

We must make peace with this associative drift. But what does this look like? Let's look at an example from the poetry of Emily Dickinson. Dickinson lived her entire life in Massachusetts. Along with Walt Whitman, she is considered one of the most important American poets of the nineteenth century. She did not publish much during her lifetime, but after her death her sister discovered that she had written nearly two thousand poems. Many of these poems were published in a series of books in the late nineteenth and early twentieth centuries, but her complete poems did not appear in print until an edition edited by Thomas H. Johnson was published in 1955.[13] This poem comes from one of the early editions of Dickinson's work:

> There's a certain slant of light,
> On winter afternoons,
> That oppresses, like the weight
> Of cathedral tunes.

11. Matthew Zapruder, *Why Poetry* (New York: Ecco, 2017), 79, 80.
12. Zapruder, *Why Poetry*, 88.
13. Thomas H. Johnson, ed., *The Complete Poems of Emily Dickinson* (Boston: Little, Brown, 1960), x.

Heavenly hurt it gives us;   5
We can find no scar,
But internal difference
Where the meanings are.

None may teach it anything,
'Tis the seal, despair,—   10
An imperial affliction
Sent us of the air.

When it comes, the landscape listens,
Shadows hold their breath;
When it goes, 'tis like the distance   15
On the look of death.[14]

We could go into a lengthy and detailed analysis of this poem, but for now let's just focus on how it resists being boiled down to a single meaning.

The first stanza offers a setting: it's a New England winter afternoon, and the way the light slants is oppressive. Think about how the sunlight fades early in the winter. While light is often associated with hope or possibility, here it hurts us, though it doesn't leave a physical scar. It hurts on the inside. The slanted light is unteachable; it doesn't change. It's an overwhelming condition. Imagine the light settling into this slant as the sun begins to set and then fading as the sun sinks beneath the horizon. The poem creates a scene, mood, and sound. It raises questions such as, Why is the light oppressive? and Why is oppression associated with church music? Our default move might be to try to formulate these questions into propositional answers: perhaps Dickinson is commenting on the oppressiveness of organized religion. But the poem resists any such simplistic thesis statement. The comparison to cathedral tunes cannot be reduced to an argument about religion; it is intended to help us understand the effects of the slant of light. Does this mean the poem has nothing to say about religion? No! She could have chosen a different image for her comparison, but she chose "cathedral tunes." My point is

14. Emily Dickinson, *Poems*, ed. Mabel Loomis Todd and T. W. Higginson (Boston: Little, Brown, 1902), 106.

that the poem is not trying to give us a unified argument that can be articulated as a singular thought.

Here's where, hopefully, we're breaking new ground. It's not that we shouldn't ask what the poem means. It's that we shouldn't think of meaning as the message or main idea of the poem. In this case that's especially true because the poem cannot be reduced to a main point. It's about the feeling produced by the slant of light on winter afternoons. The feeling is entangled with pain, despair, affliction, and death, but it cannot be summed up in a single proposition. Donald E. Thackrey argues that the poem "resists definition in terms of a logical, comprehensive statement."[15] But this resistance does not signify a lack of meaning. Meaning is simply different from what we've typically been conditioned to think it is. The late critic and translator John Ciardi contends that we should ask not *what* a poem means, but *how* it means. "The concern is not to arrive at a definition and to close the book," Ciardi maintains, "but to arrive at an experience." To put our minds at rest, he tears down the entire edifice of our attitude toward poetry: "There will never be a complete system for 'understanding' or for 'judging' poetry. Understanding and critical judgment are admirable goals, but neither can take place until the poem has been experienced, and even then there is always some part of every good work of art that can never be fully explained or categorized."[16] This is, in essence, what Zapruder wanted to say to the woman who wrote him about her frustration with the "drifting experience" she had when reading poetry. What we need to make peace with is the fact that the experience of reading is, itself, the meaning of the poem. And so, it's okay if we feel a bit like we're drifting. Perhaps that's exactly what the poem wants us to do. To understand is to let the drift carry us to the worlds the poem opens up.

More Than Message Hunters

If meaning is more than message, then we must become more than message hunters. Ciardi describes message hunting as going "through

15. Donald E. Thackrey, *Emily Dickinson's Approach to Poetry*, University of Nebraska Studies (Lincoln, NE: Folcroft Library Editions, 1973), 76.
16. John Ciardi and Miller Williams, *How Does a Poem Mean?*, 2nd ed. (Boston: Houghton Mifflin, 1975), 2.

the poem with no interest except in its paraphraseable content."[17] We might say that message hunters believe they have understood the poem when they are able to put it in other words. Ciardi attempts to redirect our relationship to poetry by teaching us to ask, How does the poem mean? rather than, What does the poem mean? because when we ask *what*, we will inevitably set out on a quest for meaning as a proposition or main idea. If we ask *how*, we will turn our attention to the experience of reading the poem, to its form as much as to its content. Form and content are, in the end, inseparable, as we have seen in earlier chapters. Ciardi says that "the poem is not a statement but a performance of forces, not an essay on life but a reenactment."[18] Of course, this view requires the kind of redefinition of meaning we have pursued in this chapter. Without a new idea of what meaning is and what it means to understand, we will fall into the gravitational pull of the age-old complaint about the obscurity of poetry.

Poetry may seem obscure if you're reading it like a statement or an essay because that's not how it's meant to be read. The poet Billy Collins says when we read this way we "tie the poem to a chair with rope / and torture a confession out of it."[19] No wonder we have such a hostile attitude toward poetry! No wonder we feel like we're locked in a combative exchange in which we want information from this thing and it doesn't want to give it to us! We have to learn to feel, resee, and come to terms with the process of making peace as a form of understanding. But you may already be anticipating problems with this argument. Perhaps you might object that if meaning is not reducible to a main idea or unified proposition, then we won't be able to say for sure what a text means. You may be worried that emotion, defamiliarization, and association might lead to a world in which all readings of a text are equally valid no matter how disparate they may be. For readers in a culture raised on a strict diet of a hermeneutics of information and who typically read most things like instruction manuals, these are natural questions. In the next chapter, I'll try to answer them by making the case that just because literary texts are

17. Ciardi and Williams, *How Does a Poem Mean?*, 3.
18. Ciardi and Williams, *How Does a Poem Mean?*, 10.
19. Billy Collins, "Introduction to Poetry," in *The Apple That Astonished Paris* (Fayetteville: University of Arkansas Press, 1988), 58.

not always reducible to a single overarching idea, it does not follow that they can mean *anything*.

EXERCISE 3

Reading for Emotion, Defamiliarization, and Association

1. Read John 6:25–59.
2. Write a few lines answering each of the following questions:
   a. What emotions do you see represented in the passage?
   b. What emotions does the passage evoke in you?
   c. What familiar things, ideas, figures does the passage make unfamiliar, or strange?
   d. What other passages, personal stories, books, memories does the passage recall for you?
3. Reflect on why you think Jesus uses this figurative language, "the bread of life."
4. Pray that God would deepen your understanding of this passage.

CHAPTER FOUR

Not *Any*thing

The professor sat at the front of the classroom facing us. "It's a spectrum," he was saying. He was holding his hands up as if to signal a touchdown, arms bent at right angles at the elbows, palms facing each other about shoulder width apart. "But the spectrum is like this," he said, nodding at the distance between his palms, "not like this"—he laughed as he stretched his hands as far apart as possible. I will never forget that moment. We had been wrestling with how to read a sonnet written by William Shakespeare and arriving at a couple competing interpretations that seemed equally valid. But what became clear as Michael Travers explained that meaning, in this case, functioned like a spectrum rather than a single point was that our differing interpretations were not really competing. They weren't at odds with one another. There was enough room in the language of the poem for both to be true. His hand gestures were intended to show us two things. First, the meaning of the poem could not be reduced to a singular main idea. Second, this irreducibility was not an excuse to argue that the poem could mean *any*thing. The sonnet proffered a limited range of meanings, not an infinite range of meanings.

In the last chapter, we examined three elements of meaning beyond the typical definition of a main idea or point. But you may be wondering how this concept of meaning avoids slipping into a kind of facile relativism in which a literary text can always mean whatever it means to you, or me, or whomever. This objection is a reasonable one for those of us whose default is to search for a singular main idea. But even with a more robust theory of meaning that includes emotions, defamiliarization, and association, a literary text still cannot mean *any*thing. Psalm 23 is simply not about that feeling you get when you think there's one more step on the stairs as you climb and so you stomp down hard on the landing. It's just not a poem about the greatest home run hitters of all time. It's not concerned with the appropriate depth at which electrical lines should be buried. It does not stoke romantic love. So while we cannot reduce the poem to a single propositional truth (it contains more than one propositional truth!), we also cannot claim that it's a psalm about the origins of Santa Claus. Just because it may evoke different emotions in different readers, or even in the same reader at different times, it does not follow that Psalm 23 can mean *anything* we like. Meaning is complex, and so it is like a spectrum, but the spectrum is limited, not boundless.

We already know, intuitively, that a given text can mean different things at different times. How many times have you returned to a passage or verse and noticed something you hadn't noticed before? How many times have you heard someone say, or said yourself, that a verse has "taken on new meaning"? Are these experiences evidence of the fact that the meaning of the text has changed? Do they invalidate your earlier understanding? Or are they evidence that you have changed and come to understand dimensions of the text that you didn't understand before? In each case, a range of meanings is being communicated and understood. Consider how landmark events in your life have caused you to see familiar things in new ways. Were you wrong about what love was for all those years before you experienced your first romantic relationship, or did love take on new meanings in addition to the old ones when you fell in love for the first time? Your old understanding of love wasn't wrong. Rather, your new experience enabled you to understand dimensions of its meaning that you couldn't before. The meaning was always that expansive, and it was always there. It was always a range, and you became someone who could understand more of the range.

But how is it possible that one work, passage, line, or word of literature can conjure multiple meanings and yet not spin out of control into meaninglessness? The literary scholar Robert Alter offers one answer to this question when he argues that literary language is both "centripetal and centrifugal." A centripetal force is one that pulls something moving in a circular motion toward the center around which the circle is moving. The gravity of the earth acts as a centripetal force pulling an orbiting spacecraft toward the earth. When Alter contends that literary language is centripetal, he means that it tends to pull us "toward an imaginative center." In other words, a work of literature generally has some type of cohesion as a whole, and its language works to draw us into that cohesive meaning. Simultaneously, however, he insists that literary language is centrifugal. A centrifugal force is one that pushes out and away from a center while moving in a circular motion. Imagine one of those Gravitron rides that spin and pin riders against the walls. Alter claims that literary language is centrifugal because "it is never possible to specify definitively what the center of the text is or what it means."[1] Literary language is too complex to be reduced to a single concept—made up of too many images, metaphors, symbols, and other tropes that allow for ambiguity. A literary work does hold together with some cohesion, but that cohesion can rarely be summed up in a single idea.

While the paradoxical tension between the centripetal and centrifugal may seem to lead us away from understanding literature, I would argue that it should allow for all the elements of literariness, meaning, and understanding we've explored so far to click into place. A poem pulls us into a certain way of seeing, a certain kind of world. Many things are going on in that world, but there are also things that simply do not belong. To follow Alter's description, we might say that the language in a poem functions like the various physical laws of the poem's world, just like our own world has physical laws such as gravity, motion, and thermodynamics. Gravity means certain things are

1. Robert Alter, *The Pleasures of Reading in an Ideological Age* (New York: Simon & Schuster, 1989), 236–38.

possible or impossible on earth, but there is a wide range of actions that fall under the category of possible. For instance, we can jump off the ground, but only so high; we can leap off a high dive, but we cannot exceed a certain speed as we plummet toward the water; we can fly with the aid of an airplane, but not by flapping our arms. The laws of gravity do not dictate that only one kind of movement is possible, but they do dictate that not all kinds of movement are possible. Literature is like that. It is not reducible to a single idea, and yet poems and stories cannot simply mean whatever we'd like them to mean.

My goal in this chapter is not to make it possible for any literary text to be interpreted in diametrically opposing ways, especially in terms of its ideas or intellectual meaning. While some works of literature do hold contradictory ideas together in a productive tension, rarely are two opposing intellectual interpretations simultaneously true of the same text. My point, rather, is to help us make room for the expanded definition of meaning outlined in the previous chapter without spiraling out of control into a facile relativism that would ultimately render literature meaningless. If a work of literature can mean anything to anyone, then it's not very meaningful at all. But if a work of literature has a limited range of meaning that cannot be boiled down to a single idea, then it can be meaningful for many readers. As we learned in the last chapter, we can call this range "association," and we can conceive of meaning as both intellectual (ideas) and emotional (feelings).

The goal in expanding our theory of meaning is to avoid asking of a literary text only What does it mean? To ask only *What* does it mean? puts us in the ditch of missing out on the emotional dimensions of meaning, but to relativize meaning entirely sends us to the other side of the road and into the opposite ditch of meaninglessness. The purpose of this chapter is to keep us from overcorrecting and giving up on the meaning of literature altogether. Thus, I want to prove two basic points: (1) the language of the literary text itself is the best guide to its meaning; (2) emotion doesn't make meaning simplistically subjective. If we accept these premises, then whatever threats may seem to have been posed to the concept of meaning will be neutralized, and we will develop a more sophisticated sense of what meaning is and how understanding works.

If Not *Anything*, Then What?

Michael Robbins, though talking about the uses of poetry in general, can help us think about how meaning functions at the level of the individual poem: "Hammers," he says, "are good for lots of things—building birdhouses, bludgeoning ideological opponents, breaking down and becoming present-at-hand. But a hammer is obviously designed in such a way that certain purposes (driving nails) are more plausible than others."[2] The same can be said of a poem, or narrative, or even of a trope or metaphor found in an otherwise nonliterary text. It may open a set of questions or make you think of any number of your own personal experiences, but its meaning is not entirely dependent on what takes place in your head and heart. The meaning is a negotiation between you and the poem, and the materials you have to work with (the poem itself and what you bring to it) are the parameters of the meaning. Thus, even though you and I may bring different sets of experiences to the same text, it cannot simply mean "what it means to you" or "what it means to me," because we must always come back to the text.

When my students come to terms with the fact that poems are more interested in questions than answers, they sometimes overcorrect by offering readings that cannot be supported by the poems themselves. In other words, they may allow their emotions and associations to carry them away from the language, images, metaphors, themes, and sounds of the very thing they are reading. While the meaning of a poem may not be reducible to a single concept or proposition, there are parameters to its expansiveness. Those parameters are the materials of the text itself.

Consider the example of Psalm 23 (KJV), which I mentioned earlier:

> The LORD is my shepherd; I shall not want.
>> He maketh me to lie down in green pastures: he leadeth me beside the still waters.
>> He restoreth my soul: he leadeth me in the paths of righteousness for his name's sake.

2. Michael Robbins, *Equipment for Living: On Poetry and Pop Music* (New York: Simon & Schuster, 2017), 1.

Yea, though I walk through the valley of the shadow of death, I will fear no evil: for thou art with me; thy rod and thy staff they comfort me.

Thou preparest a table before me in the presence of mine enemies: thou anointest my head with oil; my cup runneth over.

Surely goodness and mercy shall follow me all the days of my life: and I will dwell in the house of the LORD for ever.[3]

The psalmist likens the experience of being shepherded by the Lord to lying down in "green pastures" beside "still waters." Now, each of us may have different images in our minds when we read this verse. Your green pasture may not look like mine; my still water may be a lake while yours is a small pool in a stream. The image of "green pastures" is one thing, but readers actually experience a variety of "green pastures." Does this variance mean that we are somehow unable to grasp the poem or talk about how it means? Of course not! Green pastures may signify in different ways for different readers, but it simply is not an image designed to evoke fear in this poem. Even if you hate the countryside, have terrible allergies, or have a fear of open spaces, the image cannot mean disdain, dread, or terror.

When we accept that a poem's meaning is both intellectual and emotional and that a poem is more interested in questions than answers, then we can strike the difficult balance of not reducing the poem to a singular idea but also avoiding conforming it to our own associations. Matthew Zapruder argues that we should make something like a border "between on the one hand what the poem is actually saying and suggesting, in its words on the page, and on the other what it makes each of us as readers think of for ourselves."[4] He argues that there should be room for talking about what kinds of thoughts and feelings a poem engenders in us as readers. However, he cautions that we should not conflate these private thoughts and feelings with the entire meaning of the poem. Notice that in my summation of Zapruder's case I didn't say that these thoughts and feelings have no place in understanding the poem. I said we shouldn't simply treat our own thoughts and feelings as equal to the meaning

3. I've used the KJV here because of the familiarity of this psalm in that translation.
4. Matthew Zapruder, *Why Poetry* (New York: Ecco, 2017), 111.

of the poem. These things are related but not identical. Our thoughts and feelings can help us step into the world of the poem so that we can begin to hear, see, feel, and think like it wants us to. When we enter the world of the poem, we begin to understand it. Remember: understanding doesn't only mean comprehending an intellectual idea or lesson.

Psalm 23 cannot be reduced to a lesson. It invites us into a certain way of feeling and seeing. It is a world unto itself, and we are being called to step into that world, acclimate ourselves, and feel at home there. We will experience the frustration of being unable to nail the poem down only if we try to nail the poem down. It's that drive toward a singular meaning that most directly causes us to overread or underread a poem. Have you ever had that experience? Perhaps you're sitting in class or Sunday school or Bible study and someone is trying to come up with specific meanings for specific images or metaphors in a biblical poem. Perhaps they speculate that the anointing of the poet's head with oil in Psalm 23 could symbolize a calling to holy leadership, since God instructs Moses to anoint Aaron and his sons to serve as priests in Exodus 30. How do you respond to this notion? It produces in me a thought that goes something like this: "Well, okay, maybe. But that doesn't really seem to be what the poem is doing." This interpretation overreaches. And why? Because it wants so desperately for the literary devices in the poem to be reducible to specific, singular propositions.

I do not mean to imply that specific images or figures, like the oil in Psalm 23, cannot be symbolic. What I mean to say is that a poem, even a line or an image, is never reducible to that symbolism. Muriel Rukeyser argues that "the image is the dramatic element of poetry. It is contained in the gross dramatic action of a poem, in which the characters act out their meaning. In the image, a relationship of language acts out its meaning." This may seem a bit abstract, but think of it like this: any specific image is one part of the larger whole of the poem. She continues: "A poem is not its images any more than a symphony is its themes. A poem is not its words any more than a symphony is its notes."[5] A symphony is more than the sum of its parts, and so

5. Muriel Rukeyser, *The Life of Poetry* (Ashfield, MA: Paris Press, 1996), 39.

is a poem. You've likely heard this saying before about something being "more than the sum of its parts," but what does it mean? Picture a construction site for a house. The land has been paid for; all the materials have been delivered; all the hours of labor that will be expended have already been estimated and calculated; all the permits are in a file on the dashboard of the supervisor's truck. Every single part of the building process has been accounted for. But when the house is built, it is worth more than the mere sum of those parts. In the crassest economic sense, its dollar amount will (hopefully) be more than the simple total of materials, labor, permits, and so forth. All those individual parts are worth more as a house than they are individually. More importantly, no one can live in a pile of nails and brackets. After all, that land, those materials, and those labor hours could be assembled into something unlivable.

The poet Carl Phillips explains the relation between the parts of the poem and the poem as a whole by using the analogy of a musical chord, which he defines as "several notes held simultaneously to produce a meaning that in music is called harmony; in lyric poetry, we call it resonance, which is more than just meaning—it's more like meaning with a lingering haunt to it, or (back to music), meaning with a vibrato."[6] Each note is a unique sound unto itself with its own tone, pitch, and feel. Strummed or struck together, the distinct notes form a new sound. The new sound cannot be explained by any of the individual notes, and neither is it identical to any of them alone. It can only be understood as itself, and yet each note plays a vital part. My only quibble with Phillips is his insistence that the resonance of the individual notes is "more than just meaning." I know what he means by this; he means something like what I mean when I say that a poem cannot be reduced to an idea. But I would rather include resonance as a part of meaning than claim that it is something that transcends or surpasses meaning. Meaning, as we saw in the previous chapter, is something more than the main idea in the text.

A poem is not merely the meanings of its individual images, symbols, and sounds added together. A poem is an imaginative object,

6. Carl Phillips, *Coin of the Realm: Essays on the Life and Art of Poetry* (St. Paul: Graywolf, 2004), 93.

a whole. More often than not, it's actually our desire to distill the poem down to a singular meaning that leads us into the troubling territory of wild speculation. After all, literary language is necessarily centrifugal. But if we attempt to get a sense of the poem as a whole and as a world, we're less likely to go astray in search of some ultimate main idea and thus less likely to get the poem wrong. In fact, in my experience, this quest for a main idea is what most often creates our frustration with the subjectivity of poetry in the first place. Thus, as Alter says, "We may enthusiastically concur in the proposition that there is never one 'correct' reading of a literary text; but when a reader assigns arbitrary meanings to key words or names in the text, when he or she proposes implications of social institutions invoked in the text that they never had in their historical setting, and when details provided by the narrator or by the characters in their dialogue are ignored or misrepresented, we are entitled to conclude that the reading in question is wrong."[7] The language itself provides the laws and parameters of the literary world the text creates. However, the text is not the only actor in the experience of reading. We must also account for the reader, especially given my argument that meaning is fundamentally emotional. If reading is always an interaction between text and reader, and if understanding the text involves a reader's emotions, then doesn't meaning automatically become subject to whatever any reader feels? Further, aren't our feelings notoriously unreliable? The next section sets out to resolve these difficult questions.

Emotion and Subjectivity

Emotions can be uncontrollable and explosive, and so perhaps it's no surprise that we are often suspicious of our emotions. Some philosophers have allowed their suspicion of emotion to lead them to believe that emotion and reason are entirely unrelated. In this view, emotions have no intellectual value whatsoever. They are more like bodily impulses. However, it has been much more common to recognize the intellectual dimensions of emotion as threats to reason. In

7. Alter, *Pleasures of Reading*, 228.

other words, many thinkers have acknowledged that our emotions and our reason are inseparable, but this has led them to conclude that we must try to create as much distance between them as possible because the thinking prompted by emotion is more unreliable than pure reason. You may recall our discussion of Plato's *Republic* in the introduction to this book. Plato was worried that Homer's representation of emotion in his famous epic poems would lead audiences astray. Thus, Plato banned the poets from his ideal city. But is emotion truly more unreliable than reason? After all, we all believe, or have believed, things that turn out to be untrue or based on faulty reason.

The philosopher Martha Nussbaum agrees with Plato and the larger school of thought that emotion has intellectual properties, but she disagrees with the assertion that emotion is more unreliable than reason. She goes so far as to claim that "emotions are not only not more unreliable than intellectual calculations, but frequently are more reliable, and less deceptively seductive."[8] You might be wondering, How?! Nussbaum argues that attempts to cut emotion out of our thinking are likely to distance us from the human implications and effects of our thought. After all, our emotions are central to our humanness. Like Plato, Nussbaum draws an example from Homer. She asks us to consider what Homer's *Odyssey* would have been like if Odysseus had decided to stay on the island with the goddess Calypso rather than venturing out on the dangerous journey home to reclaim his household and live out his days with his faithful wife and son. While the choice to leave a goddess and the possibility of eternal life and pleasure for certain death and the pain and loss of human existence might seem ludicrous, Nussbaum asks us to consider which story we would rather read. Wouldn't the poem have been boring if Odysseus had decided not to go home? Would we even still be reading it?

I would argue that aside from being impossible, an understanding entirely devoid of emotions would be useless for making sense of human existence. Nussbaum sees emotions as more reliable and less

8. Martha Nussbaum, *Love's Knowledge* (New York: Oxford University Press, 1990), 40.

deceptive than reason alone because a reason that works in coop-eration with emotion is not captive to the illusion that such dispas-sionate calculation is possible in the first place. Thinking without emotion is impoverished thinking. Literature thus offers philosophy a rich range of intellectual exploration because of its appeal to and evocation of emotion. In Nussbaum's judgment, "the emotions, and their accomplices, the stories, would be not just permitted, but re-quired, in a fully human philosophy."[9] An understanding that can't account for the most human elements of human being is not worth much. As we saw in the last chapter, to fully understand something, we must comprehend its full range of meaning, not merely its main idea.

Literary texts thus offer a ready-made experience for engaging meaning in its most robust form because they rely on emotion and often resist simplistic conclusions. And here is where I want to return to the metaphor of the spectrum that I began with in this chapter. Tuning in to the emotional registers of a text provides us with an-other set of guardrails as we work toward understanding what we're reading. It's one thing to know that a poem is about death, but quite another to understand how the poem wants us to feel about death, and another still to feel that way. Is the verse a stoic meditation on an unavoidable reality? Or perhaps it's written as a fearful diatribe against what seems like an unfair ending to life on earth. Or maybe it's a joyful celebration of moving from the sorrows of earthly ex-istence to an afterlife free of pain. Given these three options, the emotional tone can help us understand how we're supposed to read the poem.

To be clear, it's not simply that emotion can help us better under-stand the meaning, as if emotion was decoration or direction. The emotion is an integral element of the meaning. You might be able to explain the poem to someone who's never read it before, but if you do not feel the emotion like you articulate the theme, then your understanding is incomplete. To put it another way: without the emotional sense, the ideas of the poem can be interpreted in ways that violate the integrity of the work. Let's consider a classic example of

9. Nussbaum, *Love's Knowledge*, 389.

how emotion is integral to understanding. Here I'd like to return to
Robert Frost and a poem you may know, "The Road Not Taken":

> Two roads diverged in a yellow wood,
> And sorry I could not travel both
> And be one traveler, long I stood
> And looked down one as far as I could
> To where it bent in the undergrowth;   5
>
> Then took the other, as just as fair,
> And having perhaps the better claim,
> Because it was grassy and wanted wear;
> Though as for that the passing there
> Had worn them really about the same,   10
>
> And both that morning equally lay
> In leaves no step had trodden black.
> Oh, I kept the first for another day!
> Yet knowing how way leads on to way,
> I doubted if I should ever come back.   15
>
> I shall be telling this with a sigh
> Somewhere ages and ages hence:
> Two roads diverged in a wood, and I—
> I took the one less traveled by,
> And that has made all the difference.[10]   20

If you've never encountered these lines before, read them over a few
times. It's a very popular and misunderstood poem. People misread
the poem by focusing on the final lines and concluding that trailblaz-
ers are always ultimately rewarded for taking risks. Perhaps this is how
you read, or have read, the poem. We get to the end and too readily
conclude that because the character in the poem took the road less
traveled, things have worked out. That chance he took has paid off
and made all the difference in his life.

However, the "difference" of the last line is never clearly identified
as positive. It's true that the character took the road less traveled,

10. Robert Frost, "The Road Not Taken," Poets.org, Academy of American Poets,
accessed February 13, 2020, https://poets.org/poem/road-not-taken.

and it's true that this choice made all the difference in his life, but to say that the difference has been good is to jump to conclusions that are not necessarily suggested by the poem as a whole. In fact, if we consider the overall emotion of the poem, it seems more likely that the "difference" is not entirely positive. In the first stanza, the character recalls coming to a fork in a wooded path. Notice that he was "sorry" he couldn't travel both. He looked down one of the paths and then took the other because he believed it might have more to recommend it since it wasn't very worn down. But then he noted that both paths were about equally worn down and that both were equally covered in leaves. And here's where we come to the core reason for why he kept to his first choice: "Yet knowing how way leads on to way, / I doubted if I should ever come back." He didn't stick with his choice because it was more promising, or because it was more beautiful, or because it was better in some other way. No. He stuck with his original choice because, well, you know how life goes. Once you've started down one road, it's much easier to stay on that road than to backtrack and start all over. In the final stanza he switches his gaze from the past to the future and imagines that he'll tell this story with a sigh as the source of why his life has turned out the way it has.

The title of the poem is typically interpreted as referring to the seemingly less traveled road the speaker chooses, and the conclusion of the poem is often interpreted as an exhortation to blaze your own trail rather than follow in the footsteps of the crowd. But perhaps the title refers to the path the speaker "looked down . . . as far as [he] could / To where it bent in the undergrowth." "The Road Not Taken" seems to refer *not* to the path the speaker chose but to the path he *didn't* choose. Perhaps the sigh in the final stanza is laced with regret. Perhaps the "difference" of the final line is a difference of tragedy, resignation, or discontent. Perhaps the poem is a heavy-hearted "what-might-have-been." While I will not deny that there is some ambiguity, the overall emotional tone of the poem steers us closer to a dark rather than a light reading. The poem has been famously misread because of the American captivity to the pioneer spirit, to originality, to being an individual rather than a member of a crowd. These ideas are powerful, but the feeling of the poem is more circumspect than celebratory. Emotion helps us understand; it is the meaning and it can't simply be whatever any reader feels.

Okay, But . . .

Perhaps at this point you're thinking something like, Okay, but . . . I still need to be able to know and say what Psalm 23 means; I need to know what its meaning is. If by "means" here we have in mind the main idea or the singular command, I would ask why. Why do we need to reduce the poem to a singular propositional truth? The answer is likely, "Because it can't mean anything! It's God's Word, not ours. We can't make it say whatever we want." Of course it's God's Word! And of course we shouldn't make it say whatever we want. But perhaps the purpose of the literary portions of God's Word is not simply to tell us something, to explain, argue, or convince us of a propositional truth. So either we must stop asking what Psalm 23 means, or we have to expand our concept of meaning as I've suggested we do in the last two chapters.

Psalm 23 is not only trying to tell us something about the nature of God and our relationship with him. Psalm 23 creates an entire world we can imagine ourselves inhabiting. There is a significant difference between knowing that God is a source of comfort and being comforted by him. Psalm 23 sets out to demonstrate that God is our comforter by comforting us. Is the poem reducible to the idea/emotion of comfort, then? No! It includes images that range from lying down in green pastures to walking through the valley of the shadow of death to sitting at a table in the presence of your enemies. We can feel comforted, fearless, and humbled all at once. The poem is capacious enough for all these ideas and feelings. It's not that you can't be wrong in reading the poem. If you read the poem and walk away with a sense of pride in yourself, you've clearly misunderstood it. The poem can't mean just anything. But if your sense of understanding it is limited to drawing out theological propositions about the nature of God, or making a case for how Christians should confront the reality of death, then it's safe to say that your comprehension is incomplete. You need the emotional dimensions of meaning to understand this text, and we can rely on our emotions without spiraling into relativism.

Confronting Reservations and Hesitations

1. Read Psalm 23.
2. Write a list of at least three ideas/emotions the poem addresses.
3. Reflect on how these ideas/emotions factor into the meaning of the poem.
4. Pray that God would help your reading of his Word to stir these ideas and emotions in you.

CHAPTER FIVE

Reading with Our Guts

By now I hope we've firmly established that the Bible is more than an instruction manual, more than a source of information. It is not only a book for our brains but also a book for our hearts. Thus, we must learn how to read with our hearts. If this sounds strange, it's only because we have been so conditioned to think of ourselves as "thinking things" or "brains-on-a-stick," as James K. A. Smith describes our warped view of ourselves.[1] We have been trained to think of all serious reading as reading for information under the assumption that we are fundamentally intellectual creatures in search of the right ideas. In other words, we've been taught that we are what we think. In reality, Smith argues, it's not what we think that determines who we are. Rather, "what defines us is what we *love*."[2] What this means for Smith is that we are most deeply influenced and formed not by information but by habits, rituals, and practices, things that shape our loves and desires. His goal is not to dismiss intellect or education—Smith is a

---

1. James K. A. Smith, *You Are What You Love: The Spiritual Power of Habit* (Grand Rapids: Brazos, 2016), 3.
2. James K. A. Smith, *Desiring the Kingdom: Worship, Worldview, and Cultural Formation*, Cultural Liturgies 1 (Grand Rapids: Baker Academic, 2009), 25.

philosophy professor, after all—but to take love and desire seriously, to incorporate them into the spheres of learning that are often reserved for informational instruction. The question I want to answer in this chapter is, What would it mean to read the Bible for love and not only instruction?

Smith's notion of the human is a great start for answering this question. Following Saint Augustine (and the Bible), he insists the center of the human person is not the head but the "*kardia*—our gut or heart."[3] I've been arguing all along that the Bible is aimed at our hearts as much as our heads, and here we have a view of the human that emphasizes the heart. But if we are driven by what we love, how do we figure out what we love in the first place? Isn't it a conscious decision we make with our minds? Smith says, Not entirely. He argues that "our ultimate love is oriented by and to a picture of what we think it looks like for us to live well." This idea of "a picture" is key:

> A vision of the good life captures our hearts and imaginations not by providing a set of rules or ideas, but by painting a picture of what it looks like for us to flourish and live well. This is why such pictures are communicated most powerfully in stories, legends, myths, plays, novels, and films rather than dissertations, messages, and monographs. Because we are affective before we are cognitive (and even *while* we are cognitive), visions of the good get inscribed in us by means that are commensurate with our primarily affective, imaginative nature.[4]

Part of Smith's point is that if we are motivated by love and if our love is shaped by a picture of the good life, then it is likely that many Christians are being more deeply shaped by pictures painted for us by the world than by pictures derived from Christianity. Why? Because we have overlooked the power of habit and because we have misunderstood ourselves as driven mainly by ideas rather than by desires *and* ideas. As a result, I would argue, we've missed out on how the Bible is designed not only to teach us important information but also to provide our imaginations with the best picture of what it means to be a person.

3. Smith, *Desiring the Kingdom*, 47.
4. Smith, *Desiring the Kingdom*, 53.

I want to build on Smith's philosophy to focus specifically on how we can begin again to draw a vision of the good life from the Scriptures. If they are, in fact, literary and thus designed to fire our imaginations, then they can also furnish us with a picture to desire if we will only begin to read them like that, to read them for delight, pleasure, and love, to read them not only with our heads but also with our hearts, or guts.

To read with our guts. What a weird, perhaps even gross, thought. Of course, I don't literally mean that we should hold our Bibles up to our stomachs. Though perhaps we shouldn't shrug that idea off too quickly, given that Deuteronomy 6 exhorts the people of Israel: "These commandments . . . are to be on your hearts. . . . Tie them as symbols on your hands and bind them on your foreheads" (vv. 6, 8). Some Jewish readers today may even kiss a holy book when it falls on the floor, or even every time they pick it up. A character in Jonathan Safran Foer's novel *Extremely Loud and Incredibly Close* is remembered for how "when a book fell on the floor he kissed it."[5] I'm not necessarily advocating that we adopt this practice, but I do find it illustrative of the kind of posture we should take toward the Bible as a book for our entire selves. From the outset, we must begin to change not merely our mindset but our entire orientation toward the Scriptures.

If we're to read with our guts, then perhaps we should take seriously Eugene Peterson's exhortation to eat the Bible. Peterson wrote *Eat This Book* in an effort to put into action the strange exchange between Saint John and an angel in Revelation 10. In this chapter, John begins to write down what he hears when the angel shouts and the heavens thunder, but a voice commands him to stop writing and to take the scroll he sees in the angel's hand. When he approaches the angel and asks for the scroll, the angel gives it to him and says, "Take it and eat it. It will turn your stomach sour, but in your mouth it will be as sweet as honey." So John takes it and eats it and, sure enough, it tastes sweet but turns sour. Peterson sees in this exchange a model for reading the Scriptures: "'Eat this book': Get this book into your gut;

get the words of this book moving through your bloodstream; chew on these words and swallow them so they can be turned into muscle and gristle and bone. And he did it; he ate the book."[6] The Bible is a thing to be taken in by our heads and our hearts; it's something we're supposed to digest. We must do the hard work of reorienting ourselves toward this book. But how?

From Studying to Reading

The first practical move we can make in developing new reading habits is to stop studying the Bible. Or, to be more honest and less provocative, we should stop *only* studying the Bible, where *study* is treated as an exclusively intellectual or practical exercise. Echoing the Swiss theologian Karl Barth, Peterson says that we don't read the Bible "to find out how to get God into our lives, get him to participate in our lives. No. We open this book and find that page after page it takes us off guard, surprises us, and draws us into its reality, pulls us into participation with God on *his* terms."[7] When we study the Bible (something we definitely *should* do), we make it into an object of *our* attention. We subject it to whatever agenda or goal *we* have. And while this may be intellectually profitable and spiritually bene-ficial, it tends to be a practice where *we* set the terms.

The notion of study reminds me of the Israelites' attempts to garner God's support in battle against the Philistines in 1 Samuel 4. Verse 1 of that chapter tells us that "the Israelites went out to fight against the Philistines." Notice that it doesn't say God sent them out to fight. It just says they went out to fight. Things don't go their way that day, and so they say, "Let us bring the ark of the LORD's covenant . . . , so that he may go with us and save us from the hand of our enemies." They recruit God to help them in the battle they've chosen. How does it turn out? Not good. Although the Philistines quaver at first, they go on to defeat the Israelites *and* capture the ark of the Lord. What's crazy is that, from the Israelites' perspective, the

6. Eugene Peterson, *Eat This Book: A Conversation in the Art of Spiritual Reading* (Grand Rapids: Eerdmans, 2006), 37–38.
7. Peterson, *Eat This Book*, 6.

ark didn't "work." It didn't do what they had hoped it would do for them. And yet, in the next chapter when the Philistines place the ark in the temple of their god Dagon, Dagon's image falls down before the ark of the Lord twice. The ark wreaks so much havoc among the Philistines that they eventually return it to Israel of their own free will. I don't mean to say that we can't learn about God or even meet him personally through serious study of the Bible. Of course we can. But what I do mean to say is that he doesn't show up whenever we want him to. He cannot be fit into our plans. His ways cannot be conformed to our ways.

What's the difference between studying and reading? Studying, perhaps because of its association with schoolwork and practical application, is all too often synonymous with the mode of reading for instruction we've looked at in the preceding chapters. When we study, we set out to identify the main idea or the lesson of a text. This approach makes a lot of sense for some of the texts in the Bible, especially those predominantly nonliterary texts. But the Bible is mostly literature, and the Bible as it's been assembled tells a story, and so problems arise when we *only* "study." We have the bad habit, Peterson argues, "of extracting 'truths' from the stories we read: we summarize 'principles' that we can use in a variety of settings at our discretion; we distill a 'moral' that we use as a slogan on a poster or as a motto on our desk. We are taught to do this in our schools so that we can pass examinations on novels and plays. It is no wonder that we continue this abstracting, story-mutilating practice when we read our Bibles."[8] Peterson emphasizes the ideas, "truths," "principles," and "moral," but I want to focus on the actions he uses to distinguish studying from reading and to give us some concrete things to put into practice to help us start reading the Bible with our guts alongside our heads.

Extraction versus Immersion

We might think of extracting in two different ways. First, to extract is to remove something from where it belongs, isolating it, stranding

8. Peterson, *Eat This Book*, 48.

it in a strange environment. We extract minerals from the earth, juice from lemons, and teeth from mouths. In all these examples, we alienate the thing from its natural context. When we study the Bible, we're usually looking to identify some timeless truth in the text at hand and then to remove it from the context in which we find it so that we might apply it to our own contexts or personal lives. Second, someone or something stuck in a bad situation may need to be extracted. Maybe your cat is stuck in a tree, perhaps a group of children is trapped in a cave, or maybe you've just talked yourself into a sticky situation. In all these cases, we might use the word *extract* to describe the process of having someone rescue the cat, free the children, or save you from yourself. In this sense, when we study the Bible, we're trying to get the idea out of a complex situation. For instance, we may look at God's destruction of everyone but Noah and his family in Genesis 6–8 and think, I know God is love. But I also know that God can't abide sin. How can I get some important theological truth out of his decision to wipe out everyone on the face of the earth except Noah?

Whether we're extracting a truth from its context or from what feels like a sticky situation, extraction always runs the risk of alienating the truth from its environment. My argument is not that we should try to avoid extracting truths from the Bible altogether. I believe we should study the Bible and look to it to guide our lives today, and that will necessarily involve extracting truths from it on occasion. However, there's no reason to set about extracting truths every time we want to read the Scriptures. Plus, as we've already seen, the more literary texts of the Bible don't always lend themselves to this kind of extraction. What can we do instead?

When you want to *read* the Bible, don't try to "extract" anything from the experience. By this I mean don't open the book looking for a truth. Don't sit at your desk or table with a notebook, highlighter, and index cards. Instead of trying to pull something out of the text, try to immerse yourself in whatever you're reading. (Below, we'll come to some strategies of how to approach the Bible that will help you get in a reading mindset from the beginning.) Try this first with a story or poem. Imagine yourself in the world of the story. Maybe you're an Israelite who's just heard that the leaders are summoning the ark of the Lord to the battlefield. How do you feel? Does it give you hope, lift your spirits? Now what happens after you barely survive the ensuing fight while your friends are killed and the ark is stolen by the enemy? How do you react? Imagine learning that while the ark didn't seem to work for you, it's been rumored that the Philistines' gods are falling down before it. What's up with that? Are you confused? Encouraged? Fearful? Immerse yourself in the story. Don't ask, To what end? or For what purpose? *Read* the Bible as you would anything else designed to capture your imagination.

Summarizing/Distilling versus Slowing Down

Peterson says that we have been conditioned to "summarize 'principles'" and try to "distill a 'moral'" when we read the Bible. I want to treat the verbs "summarize" and "distill" together, because they are close in meaning. When we summarize, we hold on only to what is essential and cut away needless details. To distill something is to purify it, condense it, to get at its very essence. In both cases, whatever is being summarized or distilled is assumed to have a center, core, or heart that is surrounded by less vital parts. We can dispense with these less vital parts and just retain the heart. To summarize or distill the Bible is to read the text looking for this heart by cutting away whatever is unnecessary. Think of the classic illustration of a sculptor who sees the statue in the block of marble and creates a masterpiece by chiseling away the excess stone. When we summarize and distill the Scriptures, we are like the sculptor, cutting away the extra words and nonessential details, trying to see only the essence of the text.

As a result of this kind of reading, we produce summaries and distillations that often reduce complex ideas, emotions, events, and conflicts to sound bites. Peterson is critical of these sound bites, because we can use them "at our discretion" and because they can become "slogans" or "mottos."[9] He fears that this kind of reading makes it more possible for us to abuse, twist, and distort the Bible for our own purposes. Sticking with Peterson's own culinary metaphors (eating and so on), these kinds of readings produce hors

9. Peterson, *Eat This Book*, 48.

d'oeuvres or bite-size snacks. Constantly summarizing the Scriptures and distilling them down into finger foods makes them a little too easy to eat. Studying the Bible like this all the time is like loading up on appetizers and then being too stuffed to eat the actual meal you were intended to enjoy.

To summarize and distill is to scream, "HURRY UP!" We just want the important ideas. Get rid of all the fluff. If you want to *read* the Bible, slow down. Perhaps you've heard of the Slow Movement, popularized by Carl Honoré's book *In Praise of Slowness* and embodied in everything from Slow Food to Slow Cinema to Slow Education. Honoré argues that "we all belong to the same cult of speed."[10] The Slow Movement emphasizes the need to decelerate life's pace, to enjoy the experiences of being human, and to reorient ourselves away from speed and efficiency. One of the most relevant observations of the Slow Movement is that in cultures of speed, when we encounter a problem that would seem to slow us down, our natural reaction is not to slow down and solve the problem. Rather, what we do is (ingeniously) engineer ways to overcome the challenge without slowing our pace at all. Summarizing and distilling are ideal reading techniques for readers in a speed culture. Why slow down and chew the text when you can summarize its main points quickly, distill them down into a few sentences, and thus master the text and move on?

To read the Bible well, slow down. Is there any reason you have to read an entire testament, book, chapter, passage, or even verse today? Why are you in such a hurry? Don't approach the text already looking for the concentrated, bite-size, tattoo-length ideas and phrases. Take your time with all the parts of a passage. Don't treat any word as if it were disposable. Since you won't have to give a report later, there's no need to try to sum things up, tie things up, or write things up. Instead, you can slow down, calm down, and write things down. It's not that study is always fast; it's that the spirit of study is to cut away what's superfluous and get to what's important. The spirit of reading is to enjoy every last word.

10. Carl Honoré, *In Praise of Slowness: Challenging the Cult of Speed* (New York: HarperCollins, 2005), 3.

Abstraction versus Enchantment

When we extract, summarize, and distill, what we often do is take something particular and make it general; we take something concrete and make it abstract. Why? One reason is that we've been taught that the purpose of reading the Bible is to receive instructions for how to live, and so when we read a story about David and Jonathan or a poem about God's statutes, we are naturally inclined to convert them into lessons or ideas. We are conditioned to abstract them into ready-made concepts. Another reason why we do this is that, as Peterson says, we have the view that stories are not serious, that they are "for children and campfires. So we continuously convert our stories into the 'serious' speech of information and motivation."[11] Bible reading, for many of us, has been replaced by a more abstract Bible study. We have forgotten how to read like children read. We have lost the ability to be enchanted by what we read.

I was one of those kids who hated every minute of school my entire life. And yet, I loved to read. A living cliché, I remember getting in trouble for staying up past my bedtime reading. Although my parents were the ones to catch me under the covers with a flashlight, I blame them for this love of reading. My father read to me every night until I learned how to read for myself, and then I just carried on the practice. It was so natural to me that I honestly believed everyone read before they went to sleep at night. In fact, I remember hanging out one day with a friend in his room. I must have been eleven or twelve years old. I was sitting on his bed, and I looked up and asked in complete innocence, "Where is your reading lamp?" He looked at me as if someone had unzipped the me-suit they were wearing and now an entirely different person sat before him. "What are you talking about?" he asked. I said something like, "You know, your reading lamp, so you can read before you go to bed." To which he responded with an incredulous laugh, "I don't read." His tone said: "I don't know what you're talking about, buddy, and we can pretend like this never happened." I was dumbfounded. How could he not read?

I didn't read back then for the sake of the lesson, instruction, or ideas that lay somehow behind the book. I read because reading was a

11. Peterson, *Eat This Book*, 48.

part of my reality and I loved it. I couldn't imagine the world without reading. I didn't know that it was optional. This was naive, of course, but I didn't think about what I did for school as reading. In hindsight, this was a better philosophy of reading than the one I developed as I grew up. I'm trying to recapture it now, this ability to study *and* read. I'm trying to reopen my capacity for enchantment. If you want to *read* the Bible, and not just study it like you'd do for school, then you have to stop abstracting from it and start being enchanted by it. Instead of trying to identify the main idea in a story, embrace the labyrinth of relationships, conflicts, characters, and resolutions and the frequent lack of closure. Try picking up a story—like the one in 1 Samuel—and reading it like you would read a plot-driven mystery novel or like you would watch a show on Netflix.

Pay attention to the people, their motivations, their relationships. If the writer tells us that God voices his regret for making Saul king and then Samuel declares that God doesn't change his mind, don't immediately seize on this tension as an opportunity to philosophize and theologize about the nature of God. (You can always do that when you *study* the passage.) Rather, embrace the feeling of regret as part of the story. Consider that Saul and the people have just won a huge victory in 1 Samuel 15. Everyone is rejoicing; things are going great. But somehow this is the moment when the Lord experiences his most profound regret for giving the people what they wanted. There is a tension, an irony in this passage. Sure, we can abstract it to say something about God's nature or his ways being dramatically different from ours. Great. Awesome. Do that when you're *studying* the book. But you wouldn't do that if you were *reading* the passage like I used to read *My Side of the Mountain* with a pillow propping up the back corner of my bedspread so I could breathe under the covers, with a background hum of excitement and fingers-crossed hope that my parents wouldn't get suspicious. I just wanted to read the book. I was enchanted.

Time out. Should we want to be enchanted by what we read? Isn't that like being uncritical? Don't we need to take the Bible seriously? Believe it or not, literary critics are perhaps the most suspicious folks when it comes to enchantment. After all, literature is filled with characters whose lives have been ruined—or who at least have been turned into laughingstocks—by enchantment: Don Quixote, Emma Bovary, Paolo and Francesca.[12] The literary scholar Rita Felski summarizes our suspicion by saying that under the spell of enchantment, "the analytical part of your mind recedes into the background; your inner censor and critic are nowhere to be found. Instead of examining a text with a sober and clinical eye, you are pulled irresistibly into its orbit. There is no longer a sharp line between self and text but a confused and inchoate intermingling." But she goes on to defend this experience, in part because it provides an alternative to the posture of more critical reading, which, because of its inherent skepticism, has its own biases. Plus, she argues, "even as we are bewitched, possessed, emotionally overwhelmed, we know ourselves to be immersed in an imaginary spectacle: we experience art in a state of double consciousness."[13] Allowing ourselves to be enchanted by what we read will certainly shape our understanding differently than when we approach the text critically, but both postures have their blind spots. Wouldn't we be better suited by having both experiences rather than only one? And when have you ever been so lost in a movie or book that when it was finished, you no longer believed you were yourself or that you lived in your house, town, state, or country? Felski suggests that the benefits of enchantment far outweigh the costs, and for readers who want to love the Scriptures there is perhaps no better way to get caught up in the worlds the Bible creates for us than by reading for enchantment.

One More Strategy: Whim

Although I've just outlined three practices wrapped in attitudes that you can adopt to help you begin to *read* the Bible, there is one more strategy I find helpful. I think of this as a purpose, as in, "Daniel purposed in his heart" (Dan. 1:8 KJV). Thus, it's like a posture, or

---

12. Miguel de Cervantes, *Don Quixote*, trans. John Rutherford (New York: Penguin, 2003); Gustave Flaubert, *Madame Bovary*, trans. Francis Steegmuller (New York: Random House, 1991); Dante Alighieri, *The Divine Comedy*, trans. John Ciardi (New York: New American Library, 2003).

13. Rita Felski, *Uses of Literature* (Malden, MA: Blackwell, 2008), 55, 74.

stance, that you can adopt toward whatever you're reading, but it's also a practical action you can take and thus convert into a habit. It's quite simple, really: when you want to *read* the Bible, follow your whim. Perhaps this is something we know intuitively. In my own experience, I sometimes just want to pick up the Bible for pleasure, and so, rather than following some plan, I think to myself, "I'd really like to read a good story today," and so I turn to a book like 1 Samuel. Alan Jacobs offers a vocabulary for this strategy in his book *The Pleasures of Reading in an Age of Distraction*. Jacobs argues that if we do not allow ourselves the freedom to read at whim, we're doomed to "turn reading into the intellectual equivalent of eating organic greens, or (shifting the metaphor slightly) some fearfully disciplined appointment with an elliptical trainer of the mind in which you count words or pages the same way some people fix their attention on the 'calories burned' readout."[14] His fears echo my own about the way many Christians approach the Bible. How often is it something you do out of duty, obligation, or perhaps even guilt? You know you're supposed to read the Bible just like you know you're supposed to eat vegetables and exercise. We do these things because even though they are rarely pleasant, we have been told they are good for us. When students ask Jacobs what they *should* read, he says that he most often encourages them to read at whim; read what they want, read what interests them.

   This might sound all well and good as a plan for entertainment reading, but what about serious reading? (Of course, I've been trying to tear down this distinction between serious/entertaining for a while now!) Even more, how could this possibly apply to reading the Bible? Jacobs addresses the first question by distinguishing between *whim* and *Whim*: "In its lower-case version, whim is thoughtless, directionless preference that almost invariably leads to boredom or frustration or both. But Whim is something very different: it can guide us because it is based in self-knowledge."[15] He makes this distinction to foster a healthy relationship with books, and though he does

   14. Alan Jacobs, *The Pleasures of Reading in an Age of Distraction* (New York: Oxford University Press, 2011), 17.
   15. Jacobs, *Pleasures of Reading*, 41.

not address the Bible specifically in this context, I think this idea of Whim can be instructive for those who want to read the Scriptures with their guts. To read at Whim, as Jacobs describes it, is to read something because you need to read it, not because you have to, or because someone has told you to, or because you know you should. I mean *need* as in, "You need to read it like you need a drink when you're thirsty or you need a blanket when you're cold." Do you ever feel the need to read the Bible in this way?

Here's an example of how I've come to read at Whim: I have a great friend who is a little older than I am and interested in many of the same questions I'm interested in as a scholar. But he's also something like a big brother personally. We talk on the phone a lot. We share our work. When I'm struggling with something personal or professional, I know I can count on him to steer me in the right direction. Once, I was angry about something that was a big deal to me. I had been wronged, and there was nothing I could do about it. I just had to take it. I called him and he let me vent. I let it all out. He didn't chastise me for overreacting, though we did talk about the healthy limits of anger. After we hung up, he texted me two or three psalms in which the psalmist airs his grievances to God, such as Psalm 3:

> LORD, how many are my foes!
>   How many rise up against me!
> Many are saying of me,
>   "God will not deliver him."
>
> But you, LORD, are a shield around me,
>   My glory, the One who lifts my head high.
> I call out to the LORD,
>   And he answers me from his holy mountain. (vv. 1–4)

The psalmist had experienced the same thing I had experienced, and he had the words for it. I needed those words like I needed to let go of my anger. Now, when I find myself in a similar situation, my heart and mind go immediately to Psalm 3. Although I may be in the midst of a formal Bible study for church or for my own spiritual/ intellectual growth, I am drawn to Psalm 3 now when I'm angry, and

I find myself following my Whim to that poem out of a newfound knowledge of myself.

Studying and Reading with Purpose and Pleasure

When we *study* the Bible, we approach it with an agenda. Perhaps it's a question, a nagging doubt, a paradox presented to us by a skeptic, a historical inquiry, or a doctrinal problem. Or maybe we're participating in a Bible study for church or a Sunday school book study. The college or seminary student or the biblical scholar may spend hours in intellectual study of the Scriptures. We want the text to give *us* answers. We want it to meet *our* needs. *Reading* the Bible is different. When we *read* we're looking to get in on the action in the text. We're trying to join God's story.

Perhaps a physical analogy can help clarify the distinction: *study* is like weight training. You're trying to become stronger than you would normally be. *Reading* is more like eating. We do it to live, and yet we strive to make it pleasurable. There is nothing quite as satisfying as a good meal. What we're aiming for when we eat is the same thing we should be aiming for when we *read* the Scriptures: delight. When you eat well, you're in a better position to train. But the relationship goes both ways; when you train hard, you'll find yourself hungrier. You need both if you're going to grow spiritually and learn to love God's Word. If you will begin to *read* the Scriptures, immersing yourself in them, slowing down, allowing them to enchant you, giving in to Whim, you may just find that you've begun to open that other dimension of understanding we've been talking about, that element of understanding that is only accessible through delighting in the Scriptures.

EXERCISE 5
Reading at Whim

1. Read a passage of Scripture that stands out to you as a favorite.
2. Write a few sentences about why you enjoy this passage.
3. Reflect on the origins of your delight in this passage. Can you remember when/why you came to love it? What were the circumstances? Is your life now similar to, or different from, that moment?
4. Pray that God would grow your love for this passage and for his entire Word.

CHAPTER SIX

Delight and Instruction

Temple Scott was a trailblazing publisher in England and the United States in the late nineteenth and early twentieth centuries. Thomas Tanselle describes him as "a man whose whole life was tied up with books."[1] Though he was mostly an editor, one of the few books Scott wrote is a short pamphlet called *The Pleasure of Reading the Bible*. When Scott published this book in 1909, he was worried about many of the same things that trouble me about Bible reading today. He claims that the "freshness of the music wore off; the message alone was heard, and heard without the music." The result? "Teachers then became fanatics; soldiers dogmatics; and the people spiritually barren. Science and trade, with their siren voices, led to the worship of false gods where beauty is not; men fought for wealth and killed each other for a creed."[2] Scott sounds like a prophet, both for how he calls his own culture to account and for how he anticipates the future. When we lose a love for the Scripture and become interested

1. Thomas Tanselle, "The Thomas Seltzer Imprint," *Papers of the Bibliographical Society of America* 58, no. 4 (Fourth Quarter 1964): 386.
2. Temple Scott, *The Pleasure of Reading the Bible* (New York: Mitchell Kennerley, 1909), 7.

exclusively in its propositional truths, the Christian life becomes a matter of having the correct answers rather than loving God and neighbor.

However, despite its insight and prescience, there is a significant problem with Scott's analysis. For while he sees the literary forms of the Bible as sparks that might rekindle our enjoyment of it, he makes the following startling claim: "In dealing with this book, however, as a means of giving pleasure I must disregard its authoritative value for religion or theology." It seems we read either for pleasure or direction, but never both at once. But why? Why does Scott insist we have to pretend the Bible is not God's Word in order to enjoy it? Well, he continues, because "the religious emotion is not primarily pleasurable; nor is theology literature. The purpose of religion is directive to conduct; it is based on the existence of a definite relation between the individual and an accepted objective idea. Pleasure is directive to nothing; it is the emotion experienced from a freedom from any relation, when the individual is most himself. The two, therefore, are antithetical."[3] He argues that religion is fundamentally "directive to conduct." In other words, he believes that religion, and thus religious reading, is all about instruction. If we want to learn from the Bible, then we must approach it as individuals setting out to wrap our minds around "an accepted objective idea." By contrast, things that are pleasurable are not "directive"; that is, they are not instructive. We experience pleasure, he insists, only when we are not being directed toward some particular end. For Scott, pleasure and instruction are mutually exclusive.

And yet the Scriptures command both. The apostle Paul exhorts Timothy to "study to show [himself] approved unto God" (2 Tim. 2:15 KJV) just as surely as he tells the church in Rome that he "delight[s] in God's law" (Rom. 7:22). Is there, in fact, a conflict between letter and spirit, between head and heart, between learning and delight, as Temple Scott suggested? Or, perhaps if there is not a conflict, are the two simply separate? Is there no delight in learning nor learning in delight? While I think many readers have "read the letter" but remained "blind to the spirit—the spirit of Beauty, which is in the

3. Scott, *Pleasure of Reading the Bible*, 1–2.

Bible," as Scott insists, I disagree with his solution that we learn to delight in the Scriptures by setting aside their authority and theological import. We need not try to forget or trick ourselves into ignoring the authority of the Bible in order to find pleasure in reading it. In fact, I would argue that the authority of the book as God's Word should be a major attraction in learning how to love it. After all, the heart of the Christian life is a love of God that is predicated on his love for us, and if this is God's book, then we commune with him whenever we pick it up.

The Bible itself is the best source for making the case that delight and instruction are inextricably entangled with one another. Time after time we are given examples of people who take pleasure in God's Word, and often it is their transforming love for the Scriptures that leads them in the practical paths of righteousness. Take the opening of the Psalter as an example:

> Blessed is the one
> who does not walk in step with the wicked
> or stand in the way that sinners take
> or sit in the company of mockers,
> but whose delight is in the law of the LORD,
> and who meditates on his law day and night. (Ps. 1:1–2)

Notice that the one who avoids the wicked, sinners, and mockers does so, in part, because they delight in the law of the Lord and meditate on it. The very experiences of delight and meditation seem to play an important role in directing our steps. In direct defiance of what Temple Scott argued, pleasure does seem to have "directive" power.

I have been arguing all along that the Bible is more than an instruction manual, but my point has not been to minimize the Bible's power to instruct. My purpose has been to expand our concept and experience of instruction. I have repeatedly emphasized that the Scriptures do more than instruct our minds; they instruct our hearts as well. But our hearts are different than our heads and so require a different kind of instruction. Our hearts must be inflamed, captured, taken by a vision; they must be appealed to differently than our heads. They must be trained and habituated over time so that in moments of intellectual storm we have a trustworthy anchor. While we might normally think of our hearts as less stable than our minds, it's much easier to change our ideas than it is to change our desires. For instance, you might be persuaded by a documentary or a friend's testimony that you should change your diet and exercise more frequently, but being convinced is not the same thing as desiring to eat healthy food and go jogging. And consider the reverse: if you are someone who eats healthy food and exercises regularly to the point that these things have become ingrained in who you are, then you are likely to keep them up even when someone makes the case that your time could be better spent otherwise.

If meaning is more than message, then it stands to reason that instruction is more than information. Reading with our guts can thus be deeply instructive. We must simply learn that delight doesn't teach us by way of an outline with bullet-pointed ideas, though it may facilitate such learning. Delight instructs us by reorienting us, giving us a different perspective. But what does this look like practically? What does it mean to say that our delight in the Scriptures can teach us things? In this chapter I want to explore two different kinds of delight we experience in reading literature and how that delight can be instructive.

The Delight and Instruction of Identification

One of the greatest pleasures we can derive from reading is the experience of identification. By *identification* I mean simply that feeling of identifying with what you read, recognizing yourself in the text, seeing your world mirrored in a poem. We looked at an example of this in an earlier chapter when we talked about Robert Frost's poem "Birches." That moment when the poem conjures the image of a cup filled above the brim creates an opportunity for identification, for you as the reader to say in your heart, "I've experienced that before!" We identify with what we read when we feel as if the writer could have written this about us. In this sense, identification can be a bit self-centered. After all, what does it say about us when we seem to see ourselves in everything we read? But identification is not inherently narcissistic. It is only when we reduce everything we read to our own perspective that it becomes self-centered in a negative sense.

We can identify with a text just as we might identify with someone whose life is very different from our own. How do we do this? We typically look for points of contact, similar experiences, things in the other person's life with which we can identify. We then build on this common ground toward a broader understanding of what their life might be like. In this sense, identification can be both pleasurable (finding that you have something in common with someone whose life is different from yours) and instructive (learning how these commonalities manifest differently or lead the person to conclusions different from your own).

I would argue that these moments of identification can be both pleasurable and instructive. There's nothing quite like the experience of having a song or story perfectly put into music or words something you've always felt, or to have it make you aware of something you always knew implicitly but never made conscious to yourself. It is the special work of literary texts to be able to cultivate this kind of identification, and the special power of such identification to teach us to imagine the experiences of others. Though his primary focus is fiction, the late novelist David Foster Wallace can help us understand how the pleasures of identification can be instructive by enhancing our capacity for empathizing with others:

> I had a teacher I liked who used to say good fiction's job was to comfort the disturbed and disturb the comfortable. I guess a big part of serious fiction's purpose is to give the reader, who like all of us is sort of marooned in her own skull, to give her imaginative access to other selves. Since an ineluctable part of being a human self is suffering, part of what we humans come to art for is an experience of suffering, necessarily a vicarious experience, more like a sort of *generalization* of suffering. Does this make sense? We all suffer alone in the real world; true empathy's impossible. But if a piece of fiction can allow us imaginatively to identify with characters' pain, we might then also more easily conceive of others identifying with our own. This is nourishing, redemptive; we become less alone inside. It might just be that simple.[4]

4. David Foster Wallace and Larry McCaffery, "An Expanded Interview with David Foster Wallace," in *Conversations with David Foster Wallace*, ed. Stephen J. Burn (Jackson: University Press of Mississippi, 2012), 21–22.

For Wallace, what makes literature good, or serious, is how well it enables us to identify with its characters. He's specifically interested in identifying with suffering, but we don't have to limit our interest to pain just as we don't have to focus only on fiction.

The pleasures of such identification are numerous. We see ourselves in a scene or character and remark, "Hey, that's me!" or "I've experienced this exact same thing!" This phenomenon reminds us that others have gone through what we are going through. Though at this stage we're still focused on ourselves, we're realizing a bridge between ourselves and others. Next, we might recognize that if that experience was especially difficult, joyful, or boring for us, then it must be so for the characters and, by inference, others. We can now begin to imagine what it must be like for others to go through what we have gone through. The next thing you know, you're empathizing with someone. One great beauty of literature in its difference from everyday life is that you may be brought to a point of identifying with characters you would never get to know in real life because you wouldn't spend nearly as much time with them.

But how is this literary experience different from a psychological profile, a sociological study of another culture, or a philosophy of what it means to be human? Those kinds of texts are primarily descriptive, while literature is imaginative. Building on the argument in chapter 2, we might argue that literary texts are especially well suited for shaping us as ethical beings because, as Karen Swallow Prior contends, "through the imagination, readers identify with the character, learning about human nature and their own nature through their reactions to the vicarious experience." Although Wallace was focused on fiction and Prior emphasizes that genre at first as well, she goes on to insist that "even literature that doesn't have character or plot, such as poetry, allows for a similar kind of process: the speaker of the poem is a kind of character whose experience the reader enters into, and the unfolding of the poem in time as it is read is itself a form of plotting."[5] Poems and stories alike create worlds that readers must imagine in order to understand, and the primary way we

---

5. Karen Swallow Prior, *On Reading Well: Finding the Good Life through Great Books* (Grand Rapids: Brazos, 2018), 21.

imagine is through identification. That is, we make an unfamiliar world familiar by relating it to what is familiar to us. In doing so, we can find ourselves in close proximity to people and experiences we may not otherwise encounter.

We can even identify with characters and speakers whose lives and worlds seem very different from our own. Let's return to the example of Anne Bradstreet's poem "The Author to Her Book," discussed in chapter 2. Bradstreet was a Puritan woman who lived in the seventeenth century. She crossed the Atlantic Ocean by ship at a time when that was extremely dangerous. She wrote poems that were taken without her knowledge and published as a book without her permission. Then she wrote a poem about that experience in which she imagines that book as a baby to which she has given birth. Because I am a middle-class man living in the United States in the twenty-first century, these experiences are foreign to me. Specifically, since she sets out to capture her feelings about the book through the metaphor of motherhood, it might seem that I would be at a loss to understand the poem. After all, I am not a woman. I cannot give birth. I will never be a mother. And yet the form of the poem fires my imagination despite all these disparities. I am always especially taken with lines 13–14:

> I washed thy face, but more defects I saw,
> And rubbing off a spot still made a flaw.

I can readily identify with these experiences. Can you? Have you ever spilled something on yourself and found that all your efforts to clean the spot only made it worse? Imagine yourself at work, or out for dinner. You spill some pizza sauce or red wine or coffee on yourself. You rush to the nearest bathroom, rip paper towels from the dispenser, soak them, and dab desperately at the stain. To your horror, it seems to get worse. The harder you try to clean it, the worse the stain gets. How do you feel? Helpless. Powerless. Vulnerable. Hopeless. Your best efforts only make things worse.

If you can feel something in this range of emotion, then you can identify with Bradstreet. Just imagine how she must have felt: she labored over these poems but had no intentions of publishing them at the time. Her well-intentioned brother-in-law ("less wise than true," as she describes him) takes them without her knowledge and publishes them ("Who thee abroad, exposed to public view"). She cannot call them back. They have been made public for all the world to see, and no matter what she might do to them, she just feels like she's making the situation worse. Quoting the great poet and critic Sir Philip Sidney, Prior observes, "Since history is restricted to what was and philosophy to what could be, Sidney argues, literature exceeds both by offering a picture of what should be. And because 'the end of all earthly learning is virtuous action,' poetry is more likely than either philosophy or history to cultivate virtue."[6] While a biography of Bradstreet may evoke sympathy for her plight, this poem evokes empathy. It invites us to identify with her, regard her pain as our own, and thus enhance our capacity for empathy by strengthening our ability to imagine and regard the experiences of others, even others who may be very different from us.

The Delight and Instruction of Shock

The experience of shock is unlike any other feeling. *Shock* is not a synonym for *surprise* or *astonishment*. Though each of these words is often used in the definitions of the others, *shock* is unique for its visceral connotations. Shock is not merely the experience of the unexpected. The *New Oxford American Dictionary* notes that a shocking experience is one that is not only sudden but also upsetting and disturbing. Unlike *surprise* and *astonishment*, *shock* is also used as a medical term: "an acute medical condition associated with a fall in blood pressure." *Shock* thus has mental, psychological, emotional, and physical significance.

Shock may not be the easiest thing to define from a dictionary, but you know shock when you feel it. Consider that moment in J. R. R. Tolkien's *The Fellowship of the Ring* (or in Peter Jackson's film adaptation of the book) when the wizard Gandalf steps out on the bridge

---

6. Prior, *On Reading Well*, 22. Prior quotes Sir Philip Sidney, *A Defence of Poetry*, edited with an introduction and notes by Jan Van Dorsten (New York: Oxford University Press, 1982), 29.

of Khazad-dûm in chapter 5 of book 2 to defend the members of the
fellowship from the Balrog of Morgoth. Gandalf seems to defeat the
monster, only to have the beast's whip catch him around the ankle
as it falls into the shadows. The wizard is pulled into darkness along
with the Balrog.[7] Here, early in this epic, the wise leader of the group
is seemingly lost for good. We are more than stunned, astonished, or
surprised. These words are useful but inadequate to describe what we
feel. We are almost sick. It is as if we as readers/viewers have fallen off
a cliff as well. We are shocked. In this example, the shock is terrible
rather than joyful, but even loss, sadness, and devastation are vital
human emotions. The shock of Gandalf's fall will ultimately heighten
our exhilaration in the shock of his return when he rejoins members
of the fellowship in Fangorn Forest in *The Two Towers*. Thus, even
horrible shock can be pleasurable in its own way.

But how does shock instruct us? Shock requires us to question
ourselves, to doubt everything we take for granted. When Gandalf
falls from the bridge, the members of the fellowship must rethink
their entire plan. Likewise, readers of Tolkien's time must surely have
questioned how the story could even continue without the wizard.
Readers of today, who know the book to be the first of three volumes,
might wonder how in the world there could be two more books after
this central character is killed off. In other words, when we experience
a sudden shock, we are put in a position where we can no longer take
anything for granted. Shock has the power "to unravel the certainty
of one's own convictions," argues Rita Felski. Everything we think
we know is called into question, and we must forge our own answers
rather than relying on those supplied for us by others. Unlike a typical
challenge to our assumptions, shock destroys "our sense of equi-
librium," Felski continues; "We are left at sea, dazed and confused,
fumbling for words, unable to piece together a coherent response."[8]
It shakes us, jars us (think about the need for shock absorbers on a
car). When we are shocked, we have no witty comeback, no matter
how quick-witted we are.

7. J. R. R. Tolkien, *The Fellowship of the Ring* (New York: Ballantine, 2012),
360–72 .

8. Rita Felski, *Uses of Literature* (Malden, MA: Blackwell, 2008), 110, 113.

102   Enjoying the Bible

Literary examples of shock will, necessarily, be shocking, but
there is a range of shock value. Not all forms of shock are equally
pleasurable or equally instructive. I am not interested here in art that
is gratuitously shocking, though even literature that sets out to break
every social norm and sense of propriety for no other reason than
to shock us may, sometimes, be instructive in spite of itself. Shock
is surprising by nature, and so good examples tend to flummox our
expectations as readers as much as, if not more than, they confound characters in literature. Take Kate Chopin's story "Désirée's
Baby" as an example. First published in *Vogue* magazine in 1893, it
is the story of a young woman named Désirée who was orphaned
as a child, raised by the well-to-do Valmondé family, married to a
young man of reputation and means, and has just given birth to
their first child. Set in the antebellum South, the story is haunted
by slavery. Specifically, the mystery of Désirée's parentage and racial
heritage creates unease early on. When Madame Valmondé comes
to visit after a few weeks' absence, she is shocked by what she sees:
"'This is not the baby!' she exclaimed, in startled tones." Désirée
agrees with excitement, noting how much the child has grown and
changed in its grandmother's absence. But when Madame Valmondé
proceeds to lift the child and walk "with it over to the window
that [is] lightest," Chopin suggests to us readers that the grandmother's shock may be more about the child's skin color than his
size.[9]

Chopin plays with our expectations as she works toward the story's climax. After raising our suspicion with Madame Valmondé's
shock, she then alleviates our fears by describing how much the baby
has softened his father's "imperious and exacting nature." But as the
months go by, a change occurs in Désirée's husband. He begins to
avoid her, to stay away from home, to resume his cruelty toward his
slaves. Désirée is at a loss. One day, she sees her darling child lying
asleep while one of the slave children fans him. She looks at the two
boys side by side and exclaims, "Ah!" She calls her husband and begs
him to tell her what it means:

9. Kate Chopin, "Désirée's Baby," in *The Awakening, and Other Stories* (Cambridge: Cambridge University Press, 1996), 205.

"It means," he answered lightly, "that the child is not white; it means that you are not white."

A quick conception of all that this accusation meant for her nerved her with unwonted courage to deny it. "It is a lie; it is not true, I am white! Look at my hair, it is brown; and my eyes are gray, Armand, you know they are gray. And my skin is fair," seizing his wrist. "Look at my hand; whiter than yours, Armand," she laughed hysterically.[10]

The suspicions Chopin has cultivated in subtle ways throughout the story seem to be confirmed. Désirée's mother invites her to come home, and Armand heartlessly says he wants her to go. And yet this revelation is not the story's central shock. Chopin is not nearly done with us.

When it is revealed that Désirée's baby is of mixed race, our suspicions are confirmed, not confounded. We do not question what we thought we knew; we revel in our insightfulness even as we grieve for Désirée's and the baby's treatment and fume at Armand's viciousness, racism, and lack of compassion. The shock is yet to come. After Désirée leaves, the narrator takes us forward "some weeks later" to "a curious scene enacted" at Armand's plantation. He stands in the middle of the yard burning every last artifact of his life with Désirée and their child:

> The last thing to go was a tiny bundle of letters; innocent little scribblings that Désirée had sent to him during the days of their espousal. There was the remnant of one back in the drawer from which he took them. But it was not Désirée's; it was part of an old letter from his mother to his father. He read it. She was thanking God for the blessing of her husband's love:—
>
> "But, above all," she wrote, "night and day, I thank the good God for having so arranged our lives that our dear Armand will never know that his mother, who adores him, belongs to the race that is cursed with the brand of slavery."[11]

Like Armand, we are shocked. The unexpectedness, the suddenness of the twist in the plot is pleasurable, but the effects are deep

10. Chopin, "Désirée's Baby," 208.
11. Chopin, "Désirée's Baby," 210.

and distressing. Our hearts fall as it dawns on us, as we presume it dawns on him, that he has broken his family over the idea of being "white" when he himself is not "white" in the eyes of his own society.

The conclusion of "Désirée's Baby" is more than a shocking twist. Shock makes us begin to question everything we thought we knew. Like Armand, we knew that he was "white." But more to the point, perhaps, we knew what whiteness was. To be white was to have light-colored skin; it was a matter of melanin, of genetics, of biology. But now we must question even such a fundamental assumption that white is a descriptor of a biological condition. After all, Armand has lived his entire life up to this point as a Southern, aristocratic, white man, when, in fact, he has always been a Southern, aristocratic man of mixed race, which, in the world of the one-drop rule means that he is African American. How was it that he was able to pass as white if whiteness is a biological reality? The lightness of his skin plays a part in answering the question, but it is not the full answer. If whiteness was merely a matter of bloodlines, biology, genetics, DNA, then no person of mixed race could be white even if, like Armand, they didn't know they were of mixed race. Under this biological view of race, such a person could only pretend for so long because the ultimate reality is blood. But for all his life Armand has lived as a white man, with the powers and privileges of a white man. If he hadn't found his mother's letter, he likely would have lived that way the rest of his life. The shock of the story's ending leads us to the instructive question: What is whiteness?

Some beliefs, ideas, and habits are so deeply ingrained in us that it takes a shock just to become aware of them, let alone to reexamine them.

Gut Reading

When was the last time you were shocked by the Bible? The passion of Jesus Christ is an offensively shocking event. But I fear we have become numb to it. The disciples certainly didn't expect it; they didn't seem to believe it would really happen right up until the moment of truth. Even those who saw such things every day, like the Roman soldiers, were shocked by Christ's crucifixion. We all recall the shock of the centurion and his comrades in their exclamation, "Surely he was the Son of God!" (Matt. 27:54). Perhaps we know the stories too well. Or, more likely, we are reading them only for intellectual instruction.

We have forgotten how to read with our guts and have thus lost the ability to have our hearts plummet to our stomachs when Peter cuts off the ear of the high priest's servant, or when David sends Uriah to the front lines just as he himself had been sent to the front by Saul, or when Jael drives a tent peg through Sisera's head, or when Jesus tells his disciples that it is "hard for someone who is rich to enter the kingdom of heaven" (Matt. 19:23). Such a statement by the Teacher caused his followers to question everything they knew: "When the disciples heard this, they were greatly astonished and asked, 'Who then can be saved?'" (Matt. 19:25). If we are not shocked by the Bible—that is, by the parts intended to be shocking—then I wonder whether we truly understand it, whether we are allowing it to do the work in us it is designed to do, whether we are being changed by it.

To read the Bible for pleasure is not to miss out on its instructiveness nor to set aside its authority. Since the default for most of us is to focus on instruction and authority to the exclusion of pleasure and delight, it's probably more important to note what we miss out on when we eschew delight. After all, we are exhorted again and again to delight in God's Word, nine times in Psalm 119 alone! If you feel at a loss for how to do this, be encouraged. First, you can reread the last chapter, "Reading with Our Guts." Second, you can recognize that you already practice spiritual delight weekly if you're a regular church attender. Even if your church tends to treat the preaching of God's Word exclusively like a lecture or lesson, I assume that you also sing songs together. In the next chapter we will examine the practices of the Christian worship service as models for the kind of delightful reading we've been discussing throughout this book. My hope is that it will help you see that you are already equipped to read with your guts, and thus are more prepared to love the Scriptures than you think.

Questions for Review

1. Why did Temple Scott believe we must set aside the authority of Scripture to experience its pleasures?
2. What does it mean to identify with what you're reading?
3. What makes shock different from surprise?

CHAPTER SEVEN

Why We Worship

Have you ever wondered why we sing in church? Why do we stand together and say words while moving our voices up and down? Haven't we gathered to learn something about God, to receive wisdom, to hear a sermon or homily? Why must we sing? Perhaps it's because we need a longer service to justify getting together. After all, it would be exasperating if everyone interrupted their lives, got ready, rushed out the door, and made it to church on time just to leave fifteen to forty-five minutes later. Or perhaps it's because Christians have always sung in church. Or maybe we sing because we believe the Bible tells us to: the apostle Paul instructs the Christians at Colossae to sing, and we reason that if it was good for early Christians to sing, then it must be good for us to do so as well. While there are wildly variant views about the appropriate kinds of music, instrumentation, and presentation, there are very few Christian worship services that don't involve some form of singing.

I owe a special debt of gratitude to my colleague Benjamin Quinn and my pastor James White of Christ Our King Community Church for direction and feedback on this chapter.

It should come as no surprise by this point that my argument for why we sing stems from the conviction that we are more than minds. We sing because music gets our hearts involved in worship. If we want to appeal to Paul's teaching as a rationale for why we sing, then let's take his exhortation to the Colossians seriously: "Let the message of Christ dwell among you richly as you teach and admonish one another with all wisdom through psalms, hymns, and songs from the Spirit, singing to God with gratitude in your hearts" (Col. 3:16). First, notice how Paul emphasizes the "message of Christ," something we might assume to be information. Isn't the "message" what we encounter in sermons? And so perhaps it seems strange that Paul encourages his audience to "teach" this message and to "admonish one another" through music. He seems to value singing as an important source of teaching and admonition. What is this "wisdom" that we can learn from songs? Is there something we can learn from music that we cannot learn in the same way through hearing a sermon?

In many Christian traditions, the sermon is the most didactic portion of the worship service. In other words, the sermon is preached and viewed as the communication of information that should change what we think and how we act. But if humans are not merely brains, then it's not only our minds that need to be informed. We sing because our hearts need instruction as well. In his book *Rhythms of Grace*, Mike Cosper explains that "as we're singing and praying we're incorporating the truths of these songs and prayers in our hearts. Truth is simultaneously taught and put into action."[1] Truth is not only known; truth is felt and lived. What good is it if we know it's true that someone has been falsely convicted of a crime if we never free that person from prison or if we continue to treat them like a criminal? That would be a paltry truth. Truth *is* change in the way we live, and such change involves our heads and our hearts. Music engages us in a way sermons rarely do; it is aimed at our affections; it is pleasing to the ears.

We sing because the people of God have always known that we need to engage our emotions and imaginations in knowing God as

---

1. Mike Cosper, *Rhythms of Grace: How the Church's Worship Tells the Story of the Gospel* (Wheaton: Crossway, 2013), 118.

surely as we must put our minds to the task. God knows this as well, of course, which is why he's given us his amazing Word, a Word that appeals to our entire being. "As important as doctrine is," Cosper insists,

> as important as legal language and clear facts are, God knows we need our imaginations to be captured by truth. We need to be won over by the surpassing beauty of Christ, the utterly compelling glory of God. We must see these as a greater good and a better hope than all the promises of our idols and daydreams.
>
> So God doesn't merely present the gospel to us in a contract. He gives us a wonderfully creative book in the Bible and invites us to engage with our imagination.[2]

So if you're looking for a model, or for examples, of how to rethink Scripture as something more than an instruction manual, look no further than a Sunday morning service. Pay attention to the different elements of the service. What happens as you approach the church? What do you do when you first walk through the doors? How does the service begin? What traditions does the congregation practice weekly, monthly, quarterly, annually? In what order do the different elements of the service take place? Is that order consistent, or does it vary? Are you aware of different parts of the service, or does it all feel like one fluid event? How are the various sacraments of the Christian tradition presented and experienced? What part do you play?

Every time we lift our voices in song, greet one another, or say a benediction, we illustrate and embody the truth that, as Cosper puts it, "beliefs are both taught explicitly (through sermons and teaching) and caught implicitly (as congregations participate in the prayers and songs of the church, which are themselves loaded with affirmations and denials of beliefs)."[3] The contrast between "taught" and "caught" suggests that both the truth itself and our understanding of it cannot be reduced to mental processes. Even if you've been reading the Bible exclusively as an instruction manual, the good news is that you've likely been practicing other forms of knowing at church

2. Cosper, *Rhythms of Grace*, 184.
3. Cosper, *Rhythms of Grace*, 118–19.

every week (if you attend church) and perhaps for your entire life (if you grew up in church).

This chapter is good news! If you regularly attend a Christian worship service, then it's likely that you may already have cultivated some of the habits in your spiritual life that I've been suggesting we should practice in our reading of the Scriptures. What I want to do in this chapter is explore the connection between reading with our guts and the elements of Christian worship. In the end, I will outline a few specific strategies for how you can take practices from your experiences in church and set them in motion in your own reading of the Bible.

Thinking and Feeling in Christian Worship

A key claim I have been making throughout this book is that experience and emotion are not simply add-ons to intellectual understanding. I have insisted that a more robust reading of the Scriptures is not a matter of comprehending its main ideas and then also feeling the emotions it evokes. Rather, I have asserted that experience is *integral to* understanding, that emotions are *inseparable from* ideas and ideas *inseparable from* emotions. Another way to say it is that I have not been trying to claim that we must simply add some heart *feeling* to our head *knowledge* but to fundamentally redefine knowledge of the Bible as something that necessarily includes feeling. This redefinition of what it means to understand is a challenge for almost everyone in a post-Enlightenment world but may be especially tough for Christians in the Protestant tradition to grasp.

In most Protestant worship services, the sermon is the central event. It is the source of information while the other elements of the service (singing, the Lord's Supper, baptism, etc.) may be seen as appealing to our hearts. The centrality of the sermon is no mere accident in Protestant denominations. We honor the Scriptures as the ultimate foundation of our faith. But as Frank A. Thomas has argued, one effect of the Protestant emphasis on the teaching of Scripture is the compartmentalizing of emotion and intellect in the worship service. Sermons have largely become "rationalistic in approach and orientation, with little attention to emotional process. The goal of the sermon was to demonstrate truth, illustrate truth, logically deduce truth, and lead people to intellectually assent to truth. This by nature required an analytical, objective style that sought to impart information or give instruction."[4] The good news is that there are rich Christian traditions, even within Protestantism, that have preserved the importance of experience and emotion to understanding.

One tradition that has maintained the emotional elements of understanding alongside the intellectual elements is the African American church. Whereas white Protestant congregations in the United States have largely followed in the footsteps of their Puritan ancestors in approaching the Bible primarily as a source of divine instruction, African American congregations have built on the legacy of ancestors who needed much more than instruction from their religion. Rooted in chattel slavery, the African American church began as what Melva Wilson Costen and others have called the "Invisible Institution." Often prohibited from exercising any form of religion or vigilantly conscripted into Euro-American religious practice as a form of control, African slaves in America "developed a worship life of their own in secret places at times determined by the slave community," according to Costen. "Gatherings of the 'Invisible Institution' occurred with such frequency," she continues, "that they are considered foundational to the subsequent establishment of African American 'visible institutions': congregations, denominations, schools, burial associations, fraternal orders, sororities, political movements, and organizations for the pursuit of justice and equality."[5] There should be no surprise that a church born out of oppression and in pursuit of deliverance would find little hope in intellectualizing Christian faith. The preacher casting a vision of hope amid the evils of slavery, white supremacy, Jim Crow segregation, and mass incarceration cannot comfort people with the mere

4. Frank A. Thomas, *They Like to Never Quit Praisin' God: The Role of Celebration in Preaching* (Cleveland: United Church Press, 1997), 5.

5. Melva Wilson Costen, *African American Christian Worship*, 2nd ed. (Nashville: Abingdon, 2007), 25.

propositional truth that all humans are created in the image of God. How can such a statement be reconciled with the dramatic disparities African Americans have experienced daily?

In the African American church, even the sermon demonstrates that our ability to understand what we hear and read is as emotional as it is intellectual. "In the midst of profound anguish and suffering," Thomas explains, "the African American preacher sought not to give answers to the problem of suffering and evil in life, but to help people experience the assurance of grace in God."[6] The African American church in the United States has cultivated a robust anthropology as a result of centuries of oppression. As we've said repeatedly in these pages, humans are not only minds. We are also hearts, bodies, souls. The African American preaching tradition has had painful reasons to maintain a well-rounded view of the human—factual explanations tend to fail in the face of suffering; propositions, true as they may be, ring hollow. Thus, the point of the sermon in the African American church has historically been to provide not "abstract answers to suffering and evil, but an experience of assurance, hope, empowerment, and victory."[7] The African American preacher in America has always had to appeal to a people occupying the margins of a dominant culture designed to dehumanize them. For these reasons, African American preachers often perform in their bodies the emotions represented in the passage at hand, engage in dialogue with the congregation to ensure no one is being left behind, and preach with musical accompaniment or punctuation.

What can readers who want to love the Bible learn from the African American church's preaching traditions? We learn that the African American church in the United States is a rich repository of wisdom and a model for how Christians should imagine the relationship between head and heart. But we can also learn to identify the ways Christian worship practices in a diverse range of traditions retain rituals that teach us this truth. What truth? The truth that understanding is as emotional as it is intellectual. Or, as Thomas explains,

6. Thomas, *They Like to Never Quit Praisin' God*, 3.
7. Thomas, *They Like to Never Quit Praisin' God*, 3.

Why We Worship   113

what is traditionally known as "thinking" usually involves a significant emotional and physical distance from a thing; one objectifies
what one is thinking about, separates oneself and one's body from
it, and dissects it for clarification and analysis. But when one experiences something, the body, emotions, and thinking are significantly
involved. The body registers and confirms the reception of powerful
stimuli and responds appropriately, for example, by sweating, feeling short of breath, or blinking away tears. The response is often
automatic, below the level of conscious instruction and choice. This
is not to suggest that thinking is not part of the experiential process, but rational thinking does not dominate the process to force
abstraction and emotional distance. It is difficult to have an experience of something without thinking, but thinking that is experiential
involves the emotions and the body, deemphasizing the rigid posture
of abstraction, objectification, physical separation, and emotional
distance.[8]

In this lengthy quote, Thomas does not merely suggest that we should
think *and* feel. He points out that thinking is always a part of feeling
and vice versa. The practices of Christian worship offer concrete
examples of how we already intuitively know that thinking is a resolutely embodied, experiential, emotional phenomenon. Now let's
turn to the question of how those sacraments and practices encourage
us to worship with our guts and then, finally, consider how we can
model that kind of worshiping when reading the Scriptures.

Worshiping with Our Guts

Why do we sometimes kneel in prayer? Is kneeling merely a symbol
of submission to God? Is our posture only important insofar as it is
an outward sign of some inward state of mind? No! This physical
pose is itself a way of submitting to God. The act is submission. Our
worship services are filled with all kinds of practices—in addition to
the preaching of the Bible—by which God speaks to us and by which
we commune with him and each other. These things are not merely
decorative, just as the form of a poem is not merely decoration laid

8. Thomas, *They Like to Never Quit Praisin' God*, 36.

over its content. The sacraments in particular are themselves forms of worship. For our purposes here, what's so important about them is that they noticeably involve more of our entire selves than is typically involved in listening to a sermon in most services.

The sermon is central in many congregations, and as a Baptist I'm certainly okay with that! My point here is not to decenter the sermon. But drawing on the African American tradition, we can see how the sermon itself can function as a robust act of both intellectual and emotional communion with God. Let's focus on the sacraments, so that we can see how we are already involving our entire selves in the process of understanding. Then we can expand the scope of that kind of understanding to our reading of the Scriptures in our daily lives.

Geoffrey Wainwright, a longtime practitioner and professor of Christian worship, points out that God speaks to his people "by other means as well as by the spoken word." Wainwright offers up Martin Luther's view of baptism as an example of how the sacraments instituted by Christ "are believed to effect what they signify."[9] The sacrament of baptism signifies the Christian's death to sin and resurrection to new life as a result of their faith in the bodily death and resurrection of Jesus Christ on their behalf. When used as a verb, *effect* means to cause something to happen or to bring something about. So what does it mean to say that baptism effects what it signifies? Does it mean that baptism brings about our salvation, as some claim? Does it simply picture our salvation, as others argue? Is it a promise of things to come, as in the baptism of infants, or a confirmation of the completed work of faith, as in believer's baptism? While not all Christian traditions attribute the same significance to the sacraments of Christian worship, perhaps Christians across those traditions can agree that the sacraments *embody* the truths we find in God's Word differently than words can. Baptism demonstrates that our salvation is not the conversion of our minds alone but of our entire selves: mind and body, heart and soul. Anytime we've participated in a worship

9. Geoffrey Wainwright, "Christian Worship: Scriptural Basis and Theological Frame," in *The Oxford History of Christian Worship*, ed. Geoffrey Wainwright and Karen B. Westerfield Tucker (New York: Oxford University Press, 2006), 11.

service in which a baptism occurred, we have witnessed the kind of gut-level experience represented in the literature of the Bible.

Every week, we involve our hearts, our guts, our bodies in understanding God when we greet one another, shake hands, hug, sing, give money, bow our heads, sit, stand, sit, stand, sit, stand, sit, stand, kneel, dance, take the Lord's Supper, say "Amen," witness baptism, weep, walk the aisle, recite Scripture, creeds, and benedictions, and participate in other rituals that embody, or put into practice, what they signify. When we stand for the reading of God's Word, we do not merely symbolize honor with our bodies; we physically honor God with our bodies.

We sing because singing gets our heads and hearts involved in crying out to God, whether in praise, lament, or love. We sing because the church has always known that we are not merely minds. We sing because the joy we find in knowing our Creator cannot be adequately articulated in words alone. In his book *For the Life of the World*, the late theologian Alexander Schmemann argues that all our "technical discussions about the Church, its mission, its methods" could only be significant "within a fundamental context, and that context is the 'great joy' from which everything else in Christianity developed and acquired its meaning." For Schmemann, "joy is not something one can define or analyze. One enters into joy."[10] The various practices and rituals of Christian worship are means of entering into joy. They are embodied actions that have different sets of limitations than words, ideas, and facts. When we bring together information and actions, we get a robust encounter with the Almighty God who speaks to us in human words but who cannot be sufficiently described, explained, or contained by them. Let's consider just three of these practices of the Christian worship service—the Lord's Supper, baptism, and singing—as examples of how we are already in the habit of involving our whole selves in the process of worshiping and knowing God. In each case, I will offer a model for how we can incorporate aspects of the worship practice into our reading of the Bible.

10. Alexander Schmemann, *For the Life of the World* (Crestwood, NY: St. Vladimir's Seminary Press, 1963), 24, 25.

The Lord's Supper

It should be obvious from the outset that the Lord's Supper is an embodied practice. We take the bread and the cup; we bite, chew, swallow, and drink. Some raise the elements while the pastor reads the Bible or recalls Jesus's exhortation to remember him. In some traditions, the elements are administered to parishioners by a priest. Perhaps at your church a plate is passed, while at mine we file out of our rows and walk up to the front of the sanctuary to take the elements and return with them to our seats to take the supper together. Can you take communion by merely thinking about eating? No! If your body has not been involved in some way, you have not taken Communion.

Why couldn't Jesus simply have commanded his disciples to remember him? Why is the command attached to the bodily necessity of eating and drinking? In Luke's version of the Last Supper, we are told that after dividing the bread, Jesus breaks it and says, "This is my body given for you; do this in remembrance of me" (Luke 22:19). He tells them that the bread *is* his body, broken for them, and that the wine *is* the new covenant in his blood, poured out for them. Jesus is not merely a symbol of God's redemption; he *is* God's redemption. His actual body and blood had to be broken and shed to accomplish our salvation. The bread and wine we eat and drink become our body and blood. They form part of the substance out of which our bodies are made. We've all heard the cliché "You are what you eat." It's cliché because it's true. And whenever we eat, some of that food becomes the stuff out of which we are made. Jesus commands his disciples to eat and drink in his memory because, like him, they are called to give themselves, their bodies, the entirety of their being to God. We have the same high calling today. To this day, Christians give thanks before meals and participate in the Lord's Supper in corporate worship. Whenever we eat the bread and drink from the cup, we should remember that every atom of our beings is God's and that we are called to worship him with all of it in memory of the Messiah, who gave all of himself for us.

Perhaps Paul had the Lord's Supper in mind when he wrote these famous words to the Corinthians: "So whether you eat or drink or whatever you do, do it all for the glory of God" (1 Cor. 10:31). Like Jesus, Paul knew that every action and atom of a Christian either glorifies or dishonors God. The very food and drink we imbibe forms the substance of our physical bodies, and those bodies can either honor or disgrace our Lord. But how does the remembrance of the Lord's Supper relate to reading the Bible? In the same way that what we eat forms the substance of our bodies, so too does what we read form the substance of our thoughts and imaginations. And so, we should read the Bible like we take the Lord's Supper. But how? Well, if what we eat naturally comes to constitute our physical selves, then it follows that what we read can come to constitute our mental and imaginative selves. Let's extrapolate from the Lord's Supper to the general act of eating. If you eat mostly junk, your body will be in bad health. If you eat mostly well, your body will likely be in good health. Of course, there are health factors that are beyond our control, but generally, if you put good things in rather than bad things, your body will thank you. The same is true when it comes to what we eat mentally and emotionally.

Perhaps we should all pause for a moment and take an inventory of the things we're mentally imbibing: television, books, films, sermons, social media, podcasts, lyrics, magazines, conversations, and so on. What percentage of your mental intake would you say is made up of God's Word? The Lord's Supper is a regular reminder that our very beings rely on the sacrifice of Jesus Christ, but it should also remind us that we are what we eat. Do you read, watch, and listen to the Bible like it's the very food that will constitute your being? There should be evidence of the Scriptures in our breath, in our stride, in our body language toward one another, in the way we listen to and embrace each other. We need to read as if our very lives depend on it, even as our bodies rely on food. Read the Bible like you eat: to live. Practically, this means we must read it every day, we must read it at regular times, we must read it for both meals and snacks, we must read it because we have to and because it gives us pleasure, we must read it well.

Baptism

I come from a Baptist tradition, and so when I talk about baptism I have immersion in mind. This perspective shapes how I think about the sacrament, but most of what I say here can apply to other traditions as well. Like the Lord's Supper, baptism both signifies something and embodies what it signifies. The waters of baptism, however they cover you, both symbolize your death, burial, and resurrection in the manner of Christ's sacrifice and actualize your baptism. By "actualize" I simply mean that it's being covered in water that makes you baptized. We are exhorted time and again throughout the New Testament to be baptized, and there can be no baptism without water. Baptism is not an idea; it is an action, and it can't happen without water. Perhaps this statement is self-evident, but I think it's instructive as a model for reading the Bible.

Because we tend to approach the Bible as an instruction manual, we often read it for its main ideas: What's the main idea in this passage? What are the themes in this chapter? What can this verse tell us about who God is? These are all great questions, of course, but they are not the sum total of what the Scriptures are designed to do. We're not supposed to read exhortations to delight without delighting or admonitions to repent without repenting. Similarly, you can't only read about, hear about, think about baptism; you must *be* baptized. There must be water involved, or else you're not baptized. When we read that we are to delight in the law of the Lord, there has to be real delight involved, or else we're not . . . well . . . delighting!

How can we use baptism as a model for an actualized reading experience? Regardless of how your Christian tradition practices baptism, the experience of being baptized is fundamentally one of giving yourself over. You place yourself, or are placed, in the hands of someone who cares for you, typically a pastor/priest/minister; this person usually explains the significance of the sacrament; the actual sacrament is performed. You play a part in the baptism, of course, but you do not baptize yourself. You are relinquished into the hands of the person baptizing you. You are subjected to the water. In the Baptist tradition, you are completely immersed, lowered into the water and raised again. Baptism by immersion is a reminder that even our Lord gave himself over to be punished for sins he did not commit so that we might be raised from the death of our sins just as he was raised from the dead.

In the same way, we can relinquish ourselves to the Scriptures. Approach the Bible as you would approach your baptism. Give yourself over to it; allow it to wash over you; give up control; let the words flow; immerse yourself, as I said in an earlier chapter. Practically, this might look like binge-watching your favorite show, but with a difference. It's like binge-watching in that it's immersive, but it's different in that you might not cover a lot of material. In other words, sometimes you may immerse yourself in a long story, but at other times you may allow just a few verses to wash over you for an extended time. If you have ever binge-watched anything, then you know it tends to happen in one of two basic ways. Sometimes, you sit down with the intention of watching an entire season of a show, and so you prepare a comfortable viewing area, get some favorite snacks, and make sure you've got the schedule clearance to get lost in the story for a while. Other times, you might sit down to watch an episode but then get sucked into the action—the next thing you know you've watched five episodes. Both ways are immersive, and both offer good models for how we can read the Bible on the model of baptism.

Have you ever planned to sit down with the Scriptures and just get lost in them? Maybe now's the time! It might be best to start with minimal expectations: thirty minutes, maybe forty-five tops. Pick an especially riveting story, maybe a favorite narrative or one with an especially twisty plot. Make some popcorn, curl up on the couch or in a comfy chair, and go for it. I often make note of passages that grab my attention or capture my interest when listening to sermons or lectures. Sometimes a preacher or scholar will talk about a familiar text in a way I've never thought about, and so I'll set a reminder on my phone or make a note to return to it later. These are the main ways I come up with passages in which to immerse myself. You might also plan one of your daily reading sessions for a time that doesn't usually bump up against another commitment. By doing this, you leave yourself the freedom to stay with a reading when it pulls you in.

Singing

I want to conclude by coming back to worship through song. Songs move us in different ways than sermons. We have always known this. In a favorite song of mine, "The Stable Song" by Gregory Alan Isakov, the opening lines appeal to our collective memory of the relation between singing and worship:

> remember when our songs were just like prayers
> like gospel hymns that you called in the air

The speaker of the song asks us to remember a time when songs and prayers were inseparable—that is, a time when songs were synonymous with prayers lifted up to the divine, invocations of reverence. Ben Lerner traces the origins of poetry in English to a shepherd named Caedmon who hides in a stable when his fellow shepherds ask him to sing. God finds Caedmon in the stable and demands a song. When Caedmon finally opens his mouth to obey, he finds that he can somehow sing beautifully.[11] Perhaps this is the "stable" Isakov references in the title of his song, or perhaps not, but in both the song and story there is an implicit and unique connection between verse and worship.

We can trace the connection between poetry and spirituality even further in history than Caedmon (poetry is universal, of course, and much older than the English language, as is the Bible). Homer's epic poem *The Odyssey* begins with the poet's plea: "Goddess of song, teach me the story of a hero."[12] One of the two great, founding works of literature in the Western world makes it clear from the beginning that verse requires divine inspiration. Songs move us in different ways than sermons do, even when the message might be identical. You might hear these verses from Psalm 139 in a sermon: "If I go up to the heavens, you are there; / if I make my bed in the depths, you are there." You might just as likely hear them in a song. What you will find is that they will affect you differently (not better or worse) in the different mediums.

Why do songs move us in ways that sermons do not? Language is limited. As we saw in the opening chapters, there are ineffable things that we simply cannot do justice to in words. How many times have you heard about something for which "words just won't suffice"? Poetry depends on the limitations of language. Matthew Zapruder

11. Ben Lerner, *The Hatred of Poetry* (New York: Farrar, Straus & Giroux, 2016), 6–7.

12. Homer, *The Odyssey*, trans. Walter Shewring (New York: Oxford University Press, 2008), 1.

explains this irony well when he says that "poetry takes this inherent limitation of the material of language . . . and turns it into a place of communion." There are things we feel but cannot express. Zapruder says that it is this very gap that makes poetry divine: "It could be said the relationship of poems to what we intuit but can never fully say makes them like prayer, that unending effort to bring someone closer to the divine, without pretending the divine could ever be fully known or understood."[13] This is why we sing songs in church. There are things we intuit or feel about God and our relationship to him that cannot be perfectly communicated in language. So we depend on the combination of words and music to get a little closer to the ineffable. As Jill Crainshaw explains,

> The worship of the faith community in its thousands of different expressions throughout the world, when it is its most authentic, is a mystery, a mystery of creation and transformation. Even in the simple act of gathering, the creative mystery is present. The age-old story of God's presence with God's people is retold in doxological conversations of laughter and tears, praise and lament; and in the actions of the gathered community, in its worship and in its praxis, the gospel story is created brand-new again. New rhythms are learned. New meanings are discovered. The community taps into a cadence of creation that has never been heard quite that way before and that will never be heard in quite that way again. A wisdom is mediated in those unrepeatable moments of communal worship that cannot be articulated within the limits of human language.[14]

Have you ever noticed that a certain song is popular at your church, that this song seems especially well suited—for whatever reason—to move your congregation? People may raise their hands at the same moment in the song each time it is sung, or the music might swell predictably at a moment of lyrical triumph. Skeptics might dismiss this as emotionalism, and it's possible that some worshipers may be looking for a feel-good moment and nothing more. Sometimes

13. Matthew Zapruder, *Why Poetry* (New York: Ecco, 2017), 13.
14. Jill Y. Crainshaw, "Embodied Remembering: Wisdom, Character, and Worship," in *Character & Scripture: Moral Formation, Community, and Biblical Interpretation*, ed. William P. Brown (Grand Rapids: Eerdmans, 2002), 386.

the skeptics are right, after all. However, it may also be the case that this song is an especially powerful invocation. This is not to say that sermons cannot move our emotions or that songs cannot impart complex theological teaching. Of course they can, and in some traditions, they do! We need both songs and sermons to be moved to worship well, and so we have both worship through music and worship through preaching in our church services.

EXERCISE 6
Worship Service Inventory

1. When you next attend church, take a brief inventory of all the conventions your congregation regularly practices, from welcoming to singing to offering.
2. Write a brief paragraph in which you analyze what these practices teach you.

EXERCISE 7
Immersive Reading

1. Set aside a block of time (between twenty and forty-five minutes) to read the Scriptures.
2. Prepare a place in which to read. Make yourself comfortable, fix a snack, whatever you would normally do to hunker down and enjoy a good book, show, or movie. Remove all distractions (e.g., phone, noise, etc.).
3. Select a passage you find interesting for a specific reason you can articulate to yourself.
4. Read! If you start to get bored or distracted, that's okay. Don't push yourself too hard the first time, but keep practicing this approach until you're able to read for longer periods.

CHAPTER EIGHT

Changing Our Approach

Each semester I teach a famous (or infamous, if you ask the students) poem in one of my classes. It was written by a poet you've undoubtedly heard of if you grew up in the United States or the United Kingdom; his name is T. S. Eliot. Eliot was born in St. Louis, Missouri, but moved to England in his early twenties. It was there that he wrote and published, with the help of his friend Ezra Pound, one of the most well-known poems of the twentieth century, *The Waste Land*.[1] This poem is not long by some standards; compared with *The Odyssey* it's short. But it is long for a lyric poem of the sort we typically encounter from Eliot's time. The poem is broken into five parts that are themselves broken into smaller fragments. It contains many different voices, lacks a singular narrative thread, and frequently shifts back and forth between different languages, including English, Latin, German, and Italian. It was written in the aftermath of World War I, and its scenes are often grim and disturbing, and when they are more lighthearted, one gets the distinct feeling that either this respite is ironic or it will not last long. In short, *The*

1. T. S. Eliot, *The Waste Land*, Poetry Foundation, accessed February 13, 2020, https://www.poetryfoundation.org/poems/47311/the-waste-land.

Waste Land is the very kind of poem most readers dread and whose presentation in classrooms around the world has taught us to ask, Why doesn't the poet just say what he means?

I ask my students to "look at all the words" of this poem before we discuss it in class. I want them to read the whole thing but not labor over every word on their first reading. It's important, when reading poetry, to get a sense of the poem as a whole, and in a long poem like *The Waste Land*, it's easy to get bogged down in pretty much every line. When we next arrive in class together, I ask the students to describe their reading experience in a word. The list we assemble invariably looks something like this:

confused
frustrated
jumbled
chaotic
disordered
exasperated
angry

Sometimes there are more or different words, but this list is fairly representative. When I ask why they felt this way, they usually respond that they couldn't follow the poem, that it was incoherent, disorganized, and evasive. I then ask how they would feel if they were left stranded out in the middle of nowhere without a map, food, water, phone, or any deep knowledge of how to navigate. What would you do, I ask, if everything you had been taught and everything you valued was of absolutely no help to you in this barren landscape? How would you feel? Well, as it turns out, the list of words we come up with to describe this imaginary experience tends to be similar to the list of words we used to describe how we feel when reading *The Waste Land*. It's almost as if Eliot crafted a poem about the modern world as a wasteland that, somehow, makes us feel exactly like we're trapped in, well, a wasteland.

If you read the poem and you feel something close to the list of emotions above, then it's safe to say that you're starting to understand the poem. My students often experience these emotions and interpret them as a sign that they *do not* understand the poem, but what I try to help them see is that this frustration is part of what it means to understand the poem. Now, of course, there's much more to the poem than this. Scholars have spent years and countless hours and pages explicating this work of art. But my point is that if you don't feel the emotion of the poem, then all the analysis in the world is not going to make much difference, because the poem is designed to enact this emotion—this feeling of being lost in a wasteland—in its readers.

What we can learn from this example is that we must change our expectations when reading poems. My students almost always think they do not understand *The Waste Land* because it frustrates them, but this is because they are trying to get past, through, beyond the experience of reading to what they think is the "real" meaning behind the words somewhere. They are, as you've probably guessed by now, looking for the message. Again, it's not that the poem is without message. *The Waste Land* has many important messages. But that's not primarily what the poem is for. So we must change our expectations when approaching poems. We must start trying to get in the emotional state of the poem and stop asking what the poem means. The second will come along if we focus our attention on the first.

If you've followed the argument of this book so far, then you may have come to the point where you're wondering, *Okay, so what do I do now?* That's exactly the right question. I've been arguing that there is a problem not with the Scriptures but with how we read them. I've also been arguing that learning how to read literature, and especially poems, can help us overcome this problem with how we read. Therefore, what should come next is a prescription for a better way to read. This prescription begins, simply enough, with the exhortation to recalibrate your expectations of the Bible, though this is much easier said than done. If my students were to approach *The Waste Land* not looking for its message but attending to the experience of reading the poem, they would read it and understand it very differently. But changing our expectations and approach is difficult; it can seem like a chicken-and-egg scenario, or a vicious circle. How can I change my expectations without knowing what I'm supposed to expect? And how can I expect different things without the right expectations? Ahhh!

In the next few short chapters, I will outline some practical steps to reorient your approach to reading the Bible. In what remains of this chapter, I want to begin this process by asking us to think about poems as being more like paintings than like prose.

Poems Are More like Paintings Than like Prose

I've already compared poems to paintings a couple times in this book, and now I want to elaborate on that comparison to help us begin to change our approach to reading the Bible. If you can learn to read a poem like you experience a painting, you'll be well on your way to cultivating a different set of expectations that you can then bring to the Bible. When you recalibrate your expectations, you'll have a different kind of reading encounter with the Scriptures, and it's my hope that it'll be the kind of encounter more likely to generate a deep and abiding love for what you read.

When I say that poems are more like paintings than like prose, I mean that poems are more like art objects, self-contained works of art, things that exist in the world. Does that sound strange or abstract? Just think about the difference between a work of philosophy that you have to read your way through in a linear fashion, from beginning to end, and a painting you can stand in front of and take in all at once or a sculpture on a pedestal you can walk all the way around. Consider a poem like Psalm 23 in contrast to an epistle like Romans. You could hang Psalm 23 on the wall and consider the whole thing as an object. That would be much harder to do with the book of Romans. The purpose in drawing this distinction is to set up a different way of "reading" these things. I put "reading" in quotation marks because while reading a painting might sound strange, I simply mean reading in the broadest sense of taking in, experiencing, interpreting. Let's consider how we might "read" a painting and then try to apply that approach to the reading of a poem and, finally, some verses from the Bible.

Stan∂ in Front of It

When I talk about approaching poems as paintings with my students, I like to look at a painting by Vincent van Gogh called *The Starry Night*. It's a very famous painting, one I love. You probably know it already, but whether you do or not, take a moment and look it up if you can. I could simply stand in front of this painting for a long time. And that's where I want to start: standing in front of the painting. I had the privilege of seeing *The Starry Night* at the Museum of Modern Art in New York City in January 2017 and then of visiting the van Gogh museum later that same year, where I was mesmerized by a host of other van Gogh paintings, some of which I found just as beautiful as, or even more beautiful than, *The Starry Night*. I would stand in front of a painting for a few minutes and let my eyes move around the canvas. I didn't really think about much at first; I just took it all in. I wasn't trying to interpret it. I wasn't even noticing anything in particular, making observations, or zeroing in on one particular feature. I just stood there with no agenda except to experience the thing.

If you want to fall in love with the Scriptures, you're going to have to spend some time standing in front of them like this. Of course, looking at words is a bit different from looking at images, but keep in mind that in literary texts, writers are often employing words to catalyze or evoke images in your imagination. Consider these lines from the poem "Eliza Harris" by Frances Ellen Watkins Harper:

> Like a fawn from the arrow, startled and wild,
> A woman swept by us, bearing a child;
> In her eye was the night of a settled despair,
> And her brow was o'ershaded with anguish and care.[2]

Can you picture a baby deer frozen and then startled by an arrow? Have you ever seen an animal running for its life, its eyes huge, its legs pumping? It explodes from its frozen position and dashes wildly. It has no sense of direction, no rationale, no plan. Its only purpose is to escape danger. That is the image Harper uses to describe Eliza

2. Frances Ellen Watkins Harper, "Eliza Harris," in *Liberator*, December 16, 1853.

Harris in this stanza. She is a woman running from slave catchers with her son in her arms, desperate for escape. Take in the whole scene all at once. Read the stanza again. Don't worry too much about any particular feature or word. Don't try to figure out why a fawn and not something else. Just stand there for a minute in front of the stanza. Read it again. Let the lines wash over you. It's not that complicated, but for most of us who have been trained to read for purpose, information, and message, it's very difficult. Just stand in front of the passage for a while.

Notice Things

The next step is to notice things. I know this sounds a little simplistic, but so much of what we notice is determined by what we've been trained to notice, and what we're trying to do right now is retrain ourselves. In one of my favorite books about writing, Verlyn Klinkenborg argues that many of us have been taught by our education to disregard what stands out to us in favor of paying attention to what we're told is important. How many times have you been discouraged from voicing your own "opinion" or from using the first-person pronoun "I" in your writing? Haven't you been tirelessly redirected to what others have said, those with authority? In this way, we are trained to ignore what we notice and to value what others notice. "But everything you notice is important," Klinkenborg insists:

> If you notice something, it's because it's important.
> But what you notice depends on what you allow yourself to notice,
> And that depends on what you feel authorized, permitted to notice
> In a world where we're trained to disregard our perceptions.[3]

Klinkenborg is primarily addressing aspiring writers, people who want to write for an audience. And so, it makes sense that they should learn how to notice interesting things, because it's the very fact that something stands out *to them* that will set their observations apart from those of others and thus give them something unique, and

3. Verlyn Klinkenborg, *Several Short Sentences about Writing* (New York: Vintage, 2012), 39.

perhaps interesting, to say. But I think this insight is useful for us as readers as well, especially since we're trying to change our approach to reading to develop a different kind of relationship with the text.

But what does it mean to notice things? Aren't we always doing that? Klinkenborg says that noticing things requires us to suspend, for at least a little while, the desire to "transmute" what we notice into words. Again, he's speaking to writers, encouraging them to hold off on trying to come up with something to say just long enough to engage with whatever they're writing about. This admonition applies to readers as well, though, because we must hold off on trying to translate what we're reading into meaning for long enough to experience the thing itself. Don't immediately try to interpret the object. Stand in front of it for a while, and then just notice some things about it. What stands out to you?

When I look at *The Starry Night*, many things stand out: the swirly sky, first of all; the weird, dark, towerlike, shrub-thing in the foreground; the church in the middle of the painting; the coziness of the town tucked in between the dark hills; the deep, dark blue of the whole thing. I notice that the shrub-thing (which we know from other paintings of the same view is a cypress tree) and the church both stick up into the sky and that the cypress tree seems to dwarf the church. This contrast gets my heart going, creating in me an ominous feeling, which, in turn, sets my mind turning and prompts me to start asking questions. But that's getting a bit ahead of ourselves, and I want to practice noticing things in "Eliza Harris" before we move on to asking questions.

Like van Gogh, Harper has composed a work of art that we can take in all at once, but one that is also made up of smaller pieces we can attend to individually. Take another look at those first two lines and pay attention to the language this time:

> Like a fawn from the arrow, startled and wild,
> A woman swept by us, bearing a child;

Notice the first word of the poem, "Like." *Like* is a comparison word; it signifies that one thing is being compared to another to help us understand better. This kind of comparison that utilizes the word *like* is called a simile. Harper is comparing Eliza's flight to that of the fawn. She is using the image of the fawn to help us see Eliza. Notice the point of view from which the narrator, or speaker, speaks. The speaker addresses the audience from a first-person perspective: "A woman swept by *us* . . ." The speaker is an eyewitness to this flight. Notice that Eliza is a grown woman with a child of her own, and yet she is compared to a fawn rather than to a doe. There are so many things to notice just in these two lines. When reading a poem like this, I will often write down such observations. Don't worry about interpreting the lines yet. Just notice things.

Ask Questions

Once I've stood in front of the work for a while and begun to notice things about it, I will inevitably begin to ask questions. Questions are vital to good reading because they show us what we do not know. Paradoxically, we cannot come to know new things without confronting what we do *not* know. The Greek philosopher Plato teaches us about the relationship between ignorance and knowledge in a story about his teacher Socrates. One day a man went to the oracle at Delphi and asked her if there was anyone wiser than Socrates. The oracle insisted that there was no one wiser. When Socrates heard this, he basically looked behind him to see if the oracle had meant someone else and wondered, *Who? Me?* Socrates was baffled that anyone would consider him to be especially wise. So he visited a few people who had reputations as wise leaders. What he discovered was that, like himself, none of them knew much worthwhile. However, there was one important difference between them. The supposedly wise man thought he knew things even when he didn't, but, as Socrates says of himself, "When I do not know, neither do I think I know; so I am likely to be wiser than he to this small extent, that I do not think I know what I do not know."[4] The foundation of knowledge, then, is ignorance.

How do questions fit into the production of knowledge out of ignorance? Reflecting on Socrates's story, the German philosopher Hans-Georg Gadamer observes that "all questioning and desire to

4. Plato, *Apology*, in *Plato: Complete Works*, ed. John M. Cooper (Indianapolis: Hackett, 1997), 21.

know presuppose a knowledge that one does not know; so much so, indeed, that a particular lack of knowledge leads to a particular question."[5] Without an awareness of what you do not know, you cannot ask the kinds of questions that can ultimately produce new knowledge. If you do not have the conscious desire to know what you do not know, you're not likely to be a very good reader. Understanding starts with ignorance, yes, but more specifically it starts with a dissatisfaction with ignorance.

What kinds of questions does *The Starry Night* evoke? To return to one of my observations, I'm always struck by the two towers of the cypress tree and the church steeple. Is the church being overshadowed? For all the blazes of light in the sky, the painting is very dark. Is the darkness creeping in on the glowing little town, or is the light of the town slowly overtaking the darkness all around? Is the warmth of the town a protection against the cold dark of the surrounding terrain, or is it being slowly snuffed out? Don't worry about answers yet. Just ask questions. Remember, we are trying to change our approach to, and thus our relationship with, what we read. If you fall back into old habits of subjugating everything to meaning in the limited sense of a main idea, theme, or message, you will preclude the manifold possibilities of the text as well as the kind of relationship that will foster the delight we've been discussing throughout this book.

What kinds of questions grow out of standing in front of and noticing things in "Eliza Harris"? Limiting the scope of inquiry to just that first stanza, I'm struck by at least a few questions. Here's the stanza again:

> Like a fawn from the arrow, startled and wild,
> A woman swept by us, bearing a child;
> In her eye was the night of a settled despair,
> And her brow was o'ershaded with anguish and care.

Picking up on the observations about comparison, why compare this grown woman carrying a baby to a fawn, or baby deer, rather than

---

5. Hans-Georg Gadamer, *Truth and Method*, revised trans. Joel Weinsheimer and Donald G. Marshall (New York: Bloomsbury T&T Clark, 2013), 374.

to a doe? This question is a version of an important kind of question you can ask of just about any literary text: How else could the text have been written? or Why is it this way instead of some other way?[6] The purpose is not simply to imagine alternatives, but to come to a better understanding of why the text might be the way it is. After all, Harper could have written, "Like a deer from the arrow, startled and wild," or "Like a doe from the arrow, startled and wild," but she didn't. She wrote, "Like a fawn from the arrow, startled and wild." What might be the significance of comparing this mother to a fawn rather than a doe?

I am also curious about this speaker. Why a first-person perspective? How would the poem, and the effect of the poem, be different if that second line left out "us" or was written "them" instead of "us"? Why might Harper want a first-person point of view? What is the difference between first and third person in this instance? It's not time to get into hypotheses quite yet, but generally, first-person speakers are a bit easier to identify with and relate to, so why are we being asked to identify with the speaker of this poem as they witness this woman fleeing with her child? This question leads us to another level of questions: questions about the intended audience, historical context, and purpose of the poem. After all, if we know that the poem was first published in William Lloyd Garrison's abolitionist newspaper *The Liberator* in the years prior to the US Civil War and likely intended to appeal to readers who may have been sympathetic to the abolition of slavery, does that affect our interpretation? But let's not rush ahead. We're still just asking questions. *Notice* how these questions have led us ever onward to bigger conceptual, formal, and historical questions about the text and about ourselves. When that happens, guess what? You're reading well! You're doing it right!

Remember, we're talking about reading literature, and literature is often focused on opening things up rather than closing them down. Poems want to raise as many questions as answers. Stories often resist neat and tidy conclusions. If you're somewhat dissatisfied with the open-ended feeling of reading this way, keep two things in mind:

---

6. I'm grateful to Anthony Cuda, who taught me how to ask this question well. Check out his work here: http://ajcuda.wp.uncg.edu/.

1. You're probably feeling that way because you've been trained/conditioned to read for information/message.
2. That dissatisfaction is a sign you're reading literature more like it's designed to be read.

As you will recall, literature has different aims than expository writing. As one of my former teachers, Michael Travers, explains, "Poetry communicates experience, not just information. . . . We read poetry to experience the essential human dimension to life, to see what is important in the human condition."[7] Literary texts in general, and poetry in particular, create worlds that fire our imaginations. These worlds are complex and intricate, like real life, and in real life there is not always a single, let alone simple, answer or conclusion.

The purpose of developing a new way of reading the Bible is not so that you can get more clearly and directly at the message of whatever passage you're reading. Please keep in mind that the goal of this book is to help you love the Scriptures more. Thus, something very important needs to be said here. The approach we're beginning to develop attempts to let the text drive our reading. But by letting the text itself drive your observations and questions, you are *not* simply allowing it to speak for itself. In fact, I have emphasized the role of noticing what *you* notice and asking the questions that come from *your* observations to help us see that there are two horizons shaping your reading of the text at this stage: the horizon of the text and your own horizon.[8] By "horizon" here, I mean perspective or point of view. The text is what it is, but you're always reading it from your perspective. I don't want to give you the impression that standing in front of the text, noticing things about it, and asking questions is somehow going to give you some God's-eye view into what it's doing and saying. But what's so great about this approach is that it can make you conscious of the very things that are shaping your perspective in the first place. As you become a more experienced reader along

7. Michael E. Travers, *Encountering God in the Psalms* (Grand Rapids: Kregel, 2003), 25.
8. The formulation "two horizons" comes from Anthony Thiselton, *The Two Horizons: New Testament Hermeneutics and Philosophical Description* (Grand Rapids: Eerdmans, 1980).

these lines, you'll begin to notice, well, what kinds of things you are
prone to notice. Then, you can question yourself as to why those
kinds of things stand out to you, and you can attend to how your
perspective tends to affect your reading. Right reading is not a matter of overcoming, or setting aside, your own perspective in favor of
that of the text at hand. Right reading is a matter of bringing those
two horizons into relation with one another.

Reading Psalm 23

Perhaps you're still wishing that I would resolve the questions I've
raised. That's a natural desire. But I'm not going to do it. Instead, I
want to spend just a brief moment reading a biblical text like we've
read *The Starry Night* and "Eliza Harris." The Bible's most famous
poem offers a perfect opportunity to recalibrate our reading because
it's a passage with which you're likely already familiar and one we've
discussed already in this book. Try standing in front of Psalm 23 for
a while:

> The LORD is my shepherd; I shall not want.
> He maketh me to lie down in green pastures: he leadeth me
>   beside the still waters.
> He restoreth my soul: he leadeth me in the paths of
>   righteousness for his name's sake.
> Yea, though I walk through the valley of the shadow of
>   death, I will fear no evil: for thou art with me; thy rod and
>   thy staff they comfort me.
> Thou preparest a table before me in the presence of mine
>   enemies: thou anointest my head with oil; my cup runneth
>   over.
> Surely goodness and mercy shall follow me all the days of my
>   life: and I will dwell in the house of the LORD forever.

Just stand (or sit) there. Take everything in for a few minutes.

Now what do you notice? I notice the point of view. It's written
from a first-person perspective, and as I read the text, I find myself
reading with the voice in the poem. That is, I find myself in the "my"

of "The Lord is *my* shepherd." I notice that the voice sometimes speaks *about* God and sometimes speaks *to* him. I notice God is described as a shepherd, and so if he's *my* shepherd, then I must be the sheep. I notice a shift in the last two verses. We seem to go from the pastures to the dining hall. I'm not a sheep anymore. I'm a person at a dinner table. I don't think the image of pouring oil on the head of a sheep would make much sense, though I do find it amusing. What do you notice? Take a few moments to jot down any other observations you might have.

Consider the questions that arise out of your observations. Why the metaphor of shepherd and sheep? Aren't sheep dumb? Why am I supposed to identify with a sheep? Why this kind of metaphor and not a simile? As we saw in "Eliza Harris," a simile is a figure of speech that compares two or more things using the words *like* or *as*. Psalm 23 doesn't use a simile; it simply says that "The Lord *is* my shepherd." Why not "The Lord is *like* a shepherd"? Why the change in voice from speaking *about* to speaking *to* God? Is there anything noticeably different about the descriptions of God versus the things said directly to him? Why does the shepherd/sheep metaphor fall away in the last two verses?

These three steps—standing in front of the text, noticing things, and asking questions—should compose your initial reading of the text. They are not intended to be comprehensive. Rather, this is how you should approach literary texts when you're sitting down to read them for the first time, or for the first time in a while. Don't worry about information, messages, answers, or even historical, cultural, or political context (yours or the text's). Those things are always in play anyway. Just try to look at the thing, notice stuff, and let what you notice guide you toward some questions. The point of ending your initial reading with questions is that you create opportunities for meditating on the Bible. I could spend hours just thinking about why the psalmist drops the shepherd/sheep metaphor. I mean, why not carry it through? You're probably so familiar with the shepherd/sheep language that you might need to pause and reflect on whether you can be moved by it. Have you really taken the time to think about what it would be like to be a sheep out in the middle of a dark valley with no good means of self-defense in a world full of wolves? Do you have any claws? No. Sharp teeth? No.

Do you have any armored plates or razor-sharp ridges on your back? No. Are you faster than a wolf? No. Is strength in numbers a comfort? No. Now, why would the psalmist use this metaphor? Consider all the times David stands alone throughout his life: alone in the fields with his sheep; alone on the battlefield with Goliath; alone in a cave hiding from Saul; alone before Nathan guilty of adultery and murder. We are often alone and vulnerable in our lives, sometimes as a result of our own mistakes. Can you think of a time when you were utterly alone, helpless, fearful of what might happen? What might it mean to relate to God as your shepherd at such times?

This kind of reading is designed to lead us to moments like this, moments of emotional, experiential encounter with the Word of God. This kind of reading is designed to cultivate a different relationship with the Scriptures, not a more certain reading (though that may accompany it). If you'll begin to read following these three steps, then you'll be ready for the remaining chapters in this book, which walk through a slightly more technical approach you can adopt once you've stood in front of the text for a while, noticed things about it, and begun to ask questions.

EXERCISE 8
Standing, Noticing, Asking

1. Pick a favorite short passage from the Bible, preferably a poem, story, or even an argument that employs figurative language.
2. Spend twelve minutes reading it in the fashion described in this chapter:
   a. Three minutes reading, rereading, looking at the passage
   b. Three minutes jotting down observations about the passage
   c. Three minutes writing out a few questions that come to mind
   d. Three minutes reflecting on these questions

CHAPTER NINE

How to Read—General Sense

The focus on understanding literature in the first part of the book was intended to call attention to and challenge our ready-made way of reading the Bible solely for information. Since literary texts are typically designed with other ends in mind, they require a different kind of reading. And since much of the Bible turns out to be literary in nature, I hope that by learning what it takes to read literature well we have become better able to read the Scriptures in a way that will instruct not only our minds but our hearts also. But all that conceptual work must be put into practice at some point. So in the previous chapter I outlined an initial approach designed to set a different tone as we sit down to read. In these last few short chapters, I turn to a method for reading the Scriptures. This method does not guarantee a correct interpretation in that restrictive sense of always leading you to a singular main idea. Rather, building on the approach explained in the last chapter, this method is intended to reorient your practical approach to reading Scripture to produce a pleasurable reading of and relationship with the text. In other words, if you practice this method you may very well come to delight in, even to love, the Bible better because you will be reading with your guts and for your life, not merely with your mind and for information. Each of the three steps I discuss in these three chapters (9–11) presumes that you've been standing in front of the text for a while, noticing things about it, and asking questions. So before you move on, you may want to review chapter 8 briefly.

The first step in this method is to read the text for its general sense. To do this well, I'm going to ask you to do something that violates the spirit of the literary text in general, and of the poem in particular as I've described and explained it throughout this book. I want you to put it in your own words, or paraphrase it. Now you should object, But the poem is not easily translatable! or maybe, Paraphrase is heresy! You're right on both counts. However, my goal in asking you to paraphrase the poem is not to arrive at its true, or deeper, meaning. Paraphrase is a heresy when the purpose is to divine what the writer "really meant to say." We are after no such thing here. This kind of paraphrase does not make us into message hunters, as John Ciardi calls them, those who go "through the poem with no interest except in its paraphraseable content."[1] We are simply trying to get into the groove of the poem, trying to position ourselves so that we can see into its world. Another way of saying this is that we're not trying to "interpret" the poem at this point, at least not in the traditional sense of interpretation as getting at the informational meaning of the text. Therefore, we need not worry too much right now about how our paraphrases might compromise the integrity of the text. We just want to put it in our own words to begin to get a general sense of what the thing is about.

General Sense of "We Wear the Mask"

Before we turn to the Scriptures, let's practice reading for general sense on Paul Laurence Dunbar's poem "We Wear the Mask." Although there will be time to dig into the background of the poet and the poem later on in the process, a little context will be helpful up front, especially if you've never heard of Dunbar. Born to two former slaves in 1872, he grew up in Ohio, where he excelled in school, but "racial

1. John Ciardi and Miller Williams, *How Does a Poem Mean?*, 2nd ed. (Boston: Houghton Mifflin, 1975), 3.

discrimination forced Dunbar to accept a job as an elevator operator in a Dayton hotel."[2] He died tragically young at the age of thirty-three in 1906. Dunbar published most of his influential poetry right at the end of the nineteenth century. In a 1925 essay, his contemporary, the poet and critic William Stanley Braithwaite, recognized Dunbar's work as "our first authentic lyric utterance, an utterance more authentic, I should say, for its faithful rendition of Negro life and character than for any rare or subtle artistry of expression."[3] "We Wear the Mask" is recognized by many critics and scholars as Dunbar's best poem.

We will get to the general sense in a moment, but first try practicing the approach outlined in the previous chapter by standing in front of this poem for a few minutes, noticing some things about it, and then asking questions. Here's "We Wear the Mask":

> We wear the mask that grins and lies,
> It hides our cheeks and shades our eyes,—
> This debt we pay to human guile;
> With torn and bleeding hearts we smile,
> And mouth with myriad subtleties.   5
>
> Why should the world be over-wise,
> In counting all our tears and sighs?
> Nay, let them only see us, while
>   We wear the mask.
>
> We smile, but, O great Christ, our cries   10
> To thee from tortured souls arise.
> We sing, but oh the clay is vile
> Beneath our feet, and long the mile;
> But let the world dream otherwise,
>   We wear the mask![4]   15

2. Joanne M. Braxton, "Paul Laurence Dunbar," in *The Concise Oxford Companion to African American Literature*, ed. William L. Andrews, Frances Smith Foster, and Trudier Harris (New York: Oxford University Press, 2001), 119.

3. William Stanley Braithwaite, "The Negro in American Literature," in *Within the Circle: An Anthology of African American Literary Criticism from the Harlem Renaissance to the Present*, ed. Angelyn Mitchell (Durham, NC: Duke University Press, 1994), 38.

4. Paul Laurence Dunbar, "We Wear the Mask," Poetry Foundation, accessed March 12, 2020, https://www.poetryfoundation.org/poems/44203/we-wear-the-mask.

Have you taken some time to orient yourself to the poem? It's impera-
tive that you be already at the question stage before you even start
our new reading method.

How should we go about putting the poem in our own words to
begin to ascertain what I'm calling its "general sense"? I suggest rewriting it.

Here's my rewrite of the first stanza of "We Wear the Mask":

We wear the mask that grins and lies,	We put on a deceptive smile
It hides our cheeks and shades our eyes,—	that hides our facial expressions,—
This debt we pay to human guile;	we owe this act to human cunning;
With torn and bleeding hearts we smile,	smiling covers up a violent and ragged wound,
And mouth with myriad subtleties.	as do many empty words.

The first stanza of "We Wear the Mask" is about African American
folks smiling through a deep and abiding pain. But this does not seem
to be a purely positive, or courageous, smile. Rather it's something
they feel they owe, like a debt they must pay.

I would paraphrase the second stanza like this:

Why should the world be over-wise,	What right do others have to know
In counting all our tears and sighs?	our pain and sorrow?
Nay, let them only see us, while	None. So only let them see
We wear the mask.	the deceptive smile.

The general sense here seems to be that it's bad enough that African
Americans must cover over their pain, so they shouldn't give the world
the satisfaction of knowing that's what they're doing.

The third and final stanza:

We smile, but, O great Christ, our cries	We smile, but dear Lord, we cry
To thee from tortured souls arise.	to you out of our suffering.
We sing, but oh the clay is vile	We sing, but the earth is revolting
Beneath our feet, and long the mile;	to the touch, and the road is long;
But let the world dream otherwise,	but let outsiders imagine things differently,
We wear the mask!	we put on the deceptive smile.

The general sense here is that the mask has been pulled back for readers to see what's going on behind it for just a moment, but it's being put back on in the end.

What is the general sense of "We Wear the Mask"? Dunbar's poem is about the deep pain that African Americans carry around with them. They hide this pain behind a mask. The poem pulls the mask off and exposes the pain just long enough for readers to realize that the mask is not an actual face, but then puts it quickly back into place. How should we interpret this pain? What is its cause? Why the reference to Christ? Who is the "world" and "them"? These questions will inevitably bubble to the surface, but for now we are only concerned with the general sense.

That's it? you may be asking! Yes. For now. My purpose is not to interpret the poem, but to try to get a general sense of what the poem is about and to begin to step into the world the poem creates. To return to an analogy I used earlier, think about what it's like when you're trying to get someone to experience a favorite song or movie the way you do but they just can't get into it. How would you go about helping them get into it? Or, think of such an example in your own life involving a favorite song or movie. Have you ever sat down to watch or listen to something you love but just not been in the right mood? You just couldn't get into the groove you need to be in to enjoy the thing? Well, what we're trying to do is get ourselves in that groove so that we can "get into" whatever it is we're reading. To do that with something new, or to do that with something familiar in a new way, you have to get the general sense of what it's

about first. I prefer to write the poem and the paraphrase out side
by side, but you do what works for you. I have already studied the
poem for a while, noticed things that stand out to me, and begun to
ask questions of it. Now I am trying to get into the way of seeing
that the poem creates.

General Sense of Psalm 119:17–24

Let's turn to Psalm 119:17–24 as we seek to put our new reading
method into practice with the Scriptures. I've chosen this text because it's easily recognizable as a poem and it explicitly exhorts us
to delight in God's Word. Take a few minutes to walk back through
the three steps outlined in the previous chapter (stand in front, notice
things, ask questions):

> [17] Be good to your servant while I live,
>   that I may obey your word.
> [18] Open my eyes that I may see
>   wonderful things in your law.
> [19] I am a stranger on earth;
>   do not hide your commands from me.
> [20] My soul is consumed with longing
>   for your laws at all times.
> [21] You rebuke the arrogant, who are accursed,
>   those who stray from your commands.
> [22] Remove from me their scorn and contempt,
>   for I keep your statutes.
> [23] Though rulers sit together and slander me,
>   your servant will meditate on your decrees.
> [24] Your statutes are my delight;
>   they are my counselors.

When I begin to let myself notice things about these verses, here's
what stands out. For starters, the psalmist talks about God's Word
in every verse! Everything in the poem revolves around God's commands. Look at all the different words used in this translation as
names for God's Word:

word

law

commands

statutes

decrees

Five different words in English are used for God's Word. Although we might say "Bible" today, the Bible as we know it now did not, of course, exist back then. But the spirit or principle translates: the speaker of the poem sees God's Word as vital to life. Everything comes back to this idea. Look, for example, at the opening lines. Why does the speaker want God to treat them well? So that life will be easy? So that they can be rich and powerful? So that they can serve God more efficiently? No, not even that! The speaker wants God to treat them well so that they will be even better able to follow God's commands.

These observations lead me to a series of questions: What exactly are God's commands? Does that mean the Ten Commandments? Is there any difference between the various words translated for God's Word, or are they basically synonyms? When you get to the question stage, it's time to put our new method into action by trying to discern the general sense of the passage. Start with a paraphrase. Here's my paraphrase of these verses:

Be good to your servant while I live, that I may obey your word.	Treat me well, Lord, so I can follow your word better.
Open my eyes that I may see wonderful things in your law.	Help me see how great your word is.
I am a stranger on earth; do not hide your commands from me.	I feel like an alien in this world; please don't keep your word from me.
My soul is consumed with longing for your laws at all times.	I ache for your word every minute of every day.
You rebuke the arrogant, who are accursed,	You correct the prideful, who

those who stray from your commands.	forsake your word.
Remove from me their scorn and contempt,	Please don't associate me with them,
for I keep your statutes.	for I follow your word.
Though rulers sit together and slander me,	Although the powerful conspire and talk badly about me,
your servant will meditate on your decrees.	I will humbly consider your word.
Your statutes are my delight;	Your words bring me joy;
they are my counselors.	they are my mentors.

The general sense of the stanza seems to be something like this: because I am a stranger in an alien and hostile land, I ache for the comfort and direction of God's Word, and when I experience it, I am filled with joy and it is as if I am no longer alone but surrounded by wise mentors.

Remember: I am not trying to arrive at the right interpretation of the verses; I am simply trying to get a general sense of what the text is about. What I'm after is not the correct paraphrase but the experience of writing it out and the effect produced by that experience. For example, the effect of writing these verses out in my own words is that I'm astounded by the single-mindedness of the psalm. It rushes through a range of fears, worries, insights, and everyday concerns but each time brings us back to God's Word. It is almost exhausting in its repetitiveness, which makes sense given the word "consumed" in verse 20. I had to keep coming up with different words for "statutes" just like the psalmist did or else repeat the same word over and over again. How many ways are there to say the same thing? Why say the same thing so many different ways? Do all of my own struggles in life always bring me back to the Scriptures?

Can you feel what's happening? I am getting into what I might describe as the zone of the poem. I am trying to put myself in a position from which I can imagine and inhabit the world the poem creates. This positioning requires a different set of questions than interpreting. Notice I'm not asking, What does the poem mean? or What is the poem's message? or What does the psalmist say about the nature of God? All of those are good questions; however, my ultimate goal right now is not interpretation but delight. My immediate purpose in ascertaining the poem's general sense is simply to step into the world it creates. I am asking what the poem is about and recognizing that it's concerned with the comprehensiveness of God's Word: its sufficiency, its ability to comfort, disrupt, and sustain me. The general sense of the poem is that the Scriptures are the very words of God. The world of the poem is one in which I am surrounded, even consumed, by God's Word.

If you're concerned at this point in the process that our interpretation will be reducible to whatever the words "mean to me," let me reassure you that we will come to context, history, convention, and form as we work through the next two steps in our method. For now, keep in mind that we are not aiming at an idea but at an experience. The psalmist (and the literary writer in general) is not merely trying to describe a scene or communicate an idea. They are rendering an experience. We must read the poem in such a way as to approximate that experience for ourselves. I've pointed out already that poets could simply expound an idea rather than writing lines of verse that seem to dance around the point. But we only think of the lines as "dancing around the point" because we're looking for (and have been taught to look for) a point in the first place. The American poet Thomas McGrath reminds us that "if the experience could be easily described perhaps it would not be necessary to write about it in poems. But the poems are discovering the experience, creating it."[5] Rewriting the lines in your own words helps you arrive at a basic understanding of the kind of experience the poem is about, the kind of experience it creates, to use McGrath's term. In other words, it gives you the most general sense of the poem.

Once you have a general sense of the poem, you will naturally want to know how you're supposed to respond to that sense. Is it a good experience? Is it bad? Are you fearful, angry, ecstatic? What kind of

5. Thomas McGrath, "Language, Power, and Dream," in *Claims for Poetry*, ed. Donald Hall (Ann Arbor: University of Michigan Press, 1982), 290.

emotion does the poem evoke? Identifying the central emotion of the poem is the next step in our method.

EXERCISE 9
General Sense

1. Read Psalm 119:25–32.
2. Rewrite the psalm in your own words.
3. Reflect on the general sense of the poem.
4. Pray to God to help you step into the world these verses imagine.

CHAPTER TEN

How to Read— Central Emotion

Once you've gotten in the groove of the literary text by reading it like a painting and getting a general sense of the world it imagines, it's time to ask an integral question. I've made the case repeatedly, and especially in chapter 3, that without pursuing this question you can't understand literature fully. The question is, What is the central emotion? Recall Helen Vendler's claim that I referenced in an earlier chapter: "The primary aim of a lyric is not to state an idea but to enact an emotion."[1] I interpret "enact" to mean that the poem is not merely trying to express an emotion but attempting to evoke it, to make it come alive in us as we read. Or we might say that the poem is not only designed to convey an emotion *to* the reader but also to enact it *in* the reader. If the primary aim of a lyric is to enact an emotion in us, then, as I've argued, we miss the point if we don't feel the emotion. If poems are designed to engender ways of feeling

1. Helen Vendler, "Author's Notes for Teaching *Poems, Poets, Poetry*," in *Poems, Poets, Poetry: An Introduction and Anthology*, ed. Helen Vendler, 3rd ed. (New York: St. Martin's Press, 2010), 4.

in us, then to understand them we will have to ask, What emotion is the text seeking to enact in me? The purpose of this chapter is to model how to read for emotional significance.

The amazing power of literature is that it enables us to experience things anew. After all, there are no new emotions, and you've probably experienced most of the emotional spectrum in your life. Who knows, perhaps you've had a wild week and run the gamut of feelings from happiness to sadness in just the last few days. Sometimes, we can even feel contradictory emotions at the same time! What makes literature, and especially poetry, so powerful is that it can enact these familiar emotions in us in new ways that make them come alive differently. As Vendler puts it, the purpose of a lyric poem is to put "a new spin on an old emotion. We call this new spin 'imagination.' To imagine the world freshly is the task of the world's artists."[2] When the psalmist expresses his contentment in Psalm 23—"The Lord is my shepherd; I shall not want"—he is not writing about an emotion that is completely alien to most of us. At some point, I imagine, we have all felt content. And yet he writes about it to imagine it anew. We read the poem in whatever circumstance we find ourselves and experience contentment once again, perhaps even as if for the first time.

Now, when Vendler talks about lyric poetry, she's talking about a very specific form of poem. For context, consider some other forms of poetry: epic, ballad, and elegy are just a few examples. Many of these forms are narrative; they have some kind of plot. While lyric poetry can contain narrative, it's usually not narrative driven. And while some narrative forms can be lyric, they tend to be too lengthy to be classified as such. I find Vendler's insights about lyric valuable for reading the Bible for two main reasons. First, much of the poetry in the Bible is closer to lyric than to other forms of poetry. The psalms, especially, read like lyrics. While they sometimes tell stories, they are more often interested in conveying the emotions of the poet. And insofar as we are intended to read them, they are brilliant and beautiful for how they give us mirrors of our own emotions and words to identify emotions we couldn't put into words ourselves. In these

2. Vendler, "Author's Notes," 5.

ways, understanding lyric is vital to reading biblical poetry. Second, what Vendler says about the primacy of emotion in lyric is useful for recalibrating our reading of all of the literary writing in the Bible, because it teaches us to pay attention to emotions and the imaginative ways they get invoked. As I've said over and over, in literature, emotion and imagination are the doorways to meaning. So although I'll follow Vendler's interest in lyric by reading a lyric poem and a lyrical passage from the Scriptures in this chapter, I hope you'll try putting this step of the process into practice with other literary texts in the Bible as well.

Central Emotion in "We Wear the Mask"

Let's stick with Dunbar's "We Wear the Mask," which we read for general sense in the last chapter, to give ourselves a consistent example to follow throughout the reading process. Here's the poem once again:

> We wear the mask that grins and lies,
> It hides our cheeks and shades our eyes,—
> This debt we pay to human guile;
> With torn and bleeding hearts we smile,
> And mouth with myriad subtleties.   5
>
> Why should the world be over-wise,
> In counting all our tears and sighs?
> Nay, let them only see us, while
>   We wear the mask.
>
> We smile, but, O great Christ, our cries   10
> To thee from tortured souls arise.
> We sing, but oh the clay is vile
> Beneath our feet, and long the mile;
> But let the world dream otherwise,
>   We wear the mask!   15

If you'll recall, the general sense of the poem is that African Americans carry a deep pain around with them, but they mask this pain with smiles and grins. The poem doesn't get into the origins or explanations for the pain; it simply conveys the pain's existence. After getting a general sense of the poem in the last chapter, we couldn't keep from jumping to questions like, How should we interpret this pain? We're still not quite there yet, but keep in mind that emotions and ideas *alike* are involved in the meaning/understanding of a poem. Be patient and attend to how asking about the poem's central emotion plays into understanding what we should do with this idea of pain.

To get a general sense of the poem, we began with paraphrase. Likewise, there are practical first steps to identifying central emotion. First, look back through your own paraphrase and note any emotion words that you used as you put the poet's language into your own words. Aim for words that convey feeling—for example, "happy," "sad," "lonely," "angry," "relieved." From my own paraphrase of "We Wear the Mask," "sorrow" and "suffering" stand out immediately. These words are not some magic key to experiencing/interpreting the poem, but taken along with the general sense, they drastically limit the ways of reading the poem. Limiting here is a good thing because it means I'm narrowing down the possible ways to experience/interpret the poem. Despite all the smiling going on, "We Wear the Mask" is simply not a joyful poem. By focusing on the emotional significance, we're eliminating whole fields of (wrong) reading and meaning.

Why did I choose these two words? I chose "sorrow" to accompany "pain" in my paraphrase of the line that reads, "In counting all our tears and sighs," which completes the thought that begins "Why should the world be over-wise, . . ." Given that the poet is describing how African Americans hide their pain (which I learned in the first stanza), it made sense to me to read "tears and sighs" as "pain and sorrow," because we shed tears when we're in pain and sighing is a sign of both sadness and resignation. You sigh when words alone fail to express your contentment, happiness, or sadness. In this case, it seemed obvious that only sadness made sense. I chose "suffering" as a way of understanding the word "tortured" in line 11. Trying to understand your paraphrase puts you in a mindset to reflect on the choices you made and to consider more deeply the language of the original poem (even if it's a translation, as any Bible you're reading in something other than Hebrew, Aramaic, or Greek will be).

Now that I've considered the main emotion words I used in my paraphrase, I'm ready to ask: Do these words capture the central emotion of the poem? Is the poem trying to enact sorrow and suffering in me? While the poem is definitely sorrowful, sorrow just doesn't seem sufficient to capture the central emotion of the entire poem. There's more to this poem than sorrow. What seems key to me is the cause of these emotions. Returning to the second stanza, where I paraphrased "tears and sighs" as "pain and sorrow," let's consider the cause of the sorrow: "Why should *the world* be over-wise . . . ?" It is a need to hide true emotions from the world that necessitates the mask and thus creates the pain of suppressing the authentic feelings. We'll return to this tension in the next chapter when we focus on the formal construction of the poem, but for now we're interested in the emotional effect. I'm not quite satisfied with "sorrow" and "suffering" as the central emotion, though I think they basically express the feeling the poem wishes to enact. These feelings are the effects of yet another, more central emotion. I want the most precise word I can find to name that central emotion, and I think that word should come from what generates the sorrow and suffering—namely, the need to hide one's true feelings. So what I'm trying to do now is come up with a good emotion word for the experience of needing to hide how I really feel. What's a good adjective to describe that need? Have you ever felt that you couldn't show your true feelings? What kind of emotion does that necessity create?

Before we identify that emotion, I want to emphasize that, while our goal in doing so is to try to understand the emotional significance of the poem, we should also be careful. We should be careful, especially when we're trying to understand a writer's representation of suffering, because we don't want to equate our own experiences with theirs even as we use our own experiences to try to understand the suffering of others. There is one sense in which suffering is a universal human experience, and yet there is another sense in which I should be vigilant not to think I can always understand others' experiences simply because I have suffered.

So what is the central emotion? I would call it something like grief-stricken defiance. You will notice that I've chosen two emotions.

That's because I don't think this poem can be neatly reduced to a singular central emotion. Instead, it seems to demand a complex, even a paradoxical, central emotion. If I were to reduce the poem to grief, I would lose sight of the strength, endurance, and persistence that stand out in the second and third stanzas. If I were to focus only on the defiance in those last two stanzas, I might miss the depths of despair that cannot be wished away by the poem's power and pride. As we'll see in the next chapter, this paradoxical emotion fits well with the poem's form as well as its historical context. Now the question is, Can you get into a way of seeing the poem that allows you to experience this grief-stricken defiance for yourself? Can you recall a time when you endured something unfair and were grieved that you couldn't show your feelings, and yet, at the same time, you were defiant, determined not to give the satisfaction of seeing you cry to those who had hurt you? Take a moment to recall such a time. Try to get in the emotional space the poem seeks to enact in you.

There might not be one good emotion word to describe that feeling, but if you have experienced it, it's possible for the poem to enact it in you. If you can't feel the emotion when reading the poem, don't get down on yourself. It's okay. Sometimes a poem will resonate strongly, and other times the same poem might not move you at all. And while it's true that some texts seem capable of moving anybody, these are works of art, and they may not be universally effective. Before moving to the biblical text, I should also briefly mention that you may have arrived at a different central emotion when reading "We Wear the Mask." There are two important things I'd like to note if that's the case for you. First, it's likely that even if we didn't arrive at the same central emotion, our emotion words will still be in the same basic part of the emotional spectrum. Second, there's room within the language of any given poem for variance. Remember, we are not trying to arrive at a singular meaning. Rather, our goal is to develop a different kind of relationship with the text, one that will draw us into reading and grow our love for reading. The only scenario in which you should worry here is if you read the poem and came to the conclusion that it enacts a wildly different emotion than the complex one I identified.

Central Emotion in Psalm 119:17–24

Psalm 119:17–24 also has a complex central emotion. As I look back through my paraphrase, the emotion words that stand out most are "feel like an alien," "ache," and "joy." These words were my paraphrases of "stranger" in verse 19, "longing" in verse 20, and "delight" in verse 24:

> [17] Be good to your servant while I live,
>   that I may obey your word.
> [18] Open my eyes that I may see
>   wonderful things in your law.
> [19] I am a stranger on earth;
>   do not hide your commands from me.
> [20] My soul is consumed with longing
>   for your laws at all times.
> [21] You rebuke the arrogant, who are accursed,
>   those who stray from your commands.
> [22] Remove from me their scorn and contempt,
>   for I keep your statutes.
> [23] Though rulers sit together and slander me,
>   your servant will meditate on your decrees.
> [24] Your statutes are my delight;
>   they are my counselors.

As with "We Wear the Mask," the central emotion is developed through the interaction between these feelings. Of course, texts can convey and enact multiple emotions. I do not want to give the impression that you've failed to understand a text if you don't arrive at a singular emotion word or phrase. We could identify multiple emotions in this stanza, but I'm trying to identify a central emotion to help me grasp the passage as a whole. It is because the psalmist feels like a stranger that he longs for God's Word, and it is only because he meditates on God's Word that he experiences delight even in the midst of this alien world. We do not have to choose one of these emotions to the exclusion of the others, but we do want to get a sense for what the verses are designed to do in us.

The psalmist is lonely. He is a stranger in a strange land. This isolation engenders an ache for comfort, which he believes can only be satisfied in God's Word. When he keeps those commands, he is made joyful. It is as if he is no longer alone but surrounded by counselors. What is a good emotion word for describing this sequence of feelings? Or, we might ask, What does it feel like to have your longing for comfort satisfied, especially when that longing is generated by feeling lonely? Or, yet another way of putting it: What is a word for having your deepest longing met? Perhaps an emotion word such as *assured* would work, but again, it seems like a phrase is in order. What about *humble confidence*? Both of these words seem necessary because the psalmist is confident, but his confidence is in God's Word, not in himself. If you are dissatisfied with my phrase, come up with your own. Remember, we are trying to come up with a name for a feeling/experience that seems inexpressible in words. That's why the poem exists in the first place! You will likely be less than happy with whatever central emotion word you decide on, because the work of literature is trying to create an imaginative experience, not tell you how to feel. Our goal is not to close the book on what the text means but to get into a certain way of seeing it.

The general sense of these verses from Psalm 119 is that God's Word provides us with comfort and guidance when we long for direction in this strange and hostile world. The feeling that results from reading the psalm is something like the humble confidence that we should experience from having that longing fulfilled. Can you recall a time when you felt utterly alone? Perhaps you were surrounded by people who misunderstood you and spoke badly of you, and you felt as if you had nowhere to turn and no one who truly understood. How badly did you long for wisdom, reassurance, guidance? How did you feel when someone stepped in to offer those things? Has anyone ever stepped into your life at a moment of desolation and given you everything you needed? How do you feel toward that person? How did you feel when the loneliness and confusion were gone? That's the central emotion the psalm wants to evoke, and not just in general. The psalmist wants to enact that emotion in you toward God's commands. The psalm wants you to feel those things for the Scriptures.

While we will finally turn to form in the next chapter, let me once again reassure you here that our goal is not to reduce the significance of the text to whatever it "makes me feel." At the same time, keep in mind that our purpose in these chapters on how to read is not to arrive at the singular intellectual meaning of whatever text we're reading. Literature seeks to fire our imaginations, and, in the process, it may teach us all kinds of things, but it is typically designed to create an imaginative experience. Because it aims at our imaginations, it is not merely trying to teach us information in the sense of data, facts, or mental knowledge. Literature, and especially poetry, has the power to enact emotions in us, to make us feel differently than we did when we first started reading, or listening. Consider that statement! Simply by looking at squiggly marks on a piece of paper, you can actually have a feeling in your innermost being! One minute you're sitting there holding some bound paper, the next you're experiencing a deep comfort, or you're crying, or you're laughing aloud alone in the room. But you don't have to stifle laughter when reading a poem about the death of a child. Likewise, you won't likely find yourself fuming with fury when experiencing the humble confidence of Psalm 119:17–24. In other words, focusing on emotion doesn't have to lead to the overstep of reducing the text to whatever we feel. Emotions are as integral to the process of understanding as are ideas, especially when it comes to understanding literature. In the next chapter, we will turn to the question that brings further context into our reading process and will provide a more complete picture of how ideas and emotions, the head and the heart, work together to produce the kind of delight that I insist is vital to understanding God's Word.

EXERCISE 10
Central Emotion

1. Read Psalm 119:25–32.
2. Write a list of words representing the emotions you see in the poem.
3. Reflect on what might be the central emotion of the poem.
4. Pray to God to help you feel the central emotion of the verses.

CHAPTER ELEVEN

How to Read—Formal Means

If you've been able to get a general sense of the world a text imagines and experience the emotion(s) it seeks to enact in you, you may very well already be delighted. But if you want to deepen that delight and fully understand both *what* and *how* the text means, then you'll need to ask one more question: Through what formal means has the text enacted that emotion in me? To put it another way, if you've been swept up into the imaginative world of a work of literature and found yourself moved by it, then you'll want to know *how* it has managed to affect you so deeply. Understanding the *how* will bring your head and your heart together. The question of *how* is a question of form: What is it about the design, structure, arrangement of the text that produces certain reading experiences to the exclusion of others? Whereas you don't need much beyond a reasonable command of the language in which a text is written to get a sense of it and to feel its emotions, understanding *how* it accomplishes those things will require a bit more work. The basic idea is that you're looking for specific elements of form in the text that produce the kind of experience you have when reading it. The good news, then, is that the concept of formal means is simple. The challenge is that the elements of literary form (e.g., metaphor, diction, imagery, parallelism, meter, allegory, genre) are not things most people think much about daily; they constitute a specialized, or technical, body of knowledge usually of interest to literary and biblical scholars. But don't worry! With just a little study and practice, you can learn enough about formal features to dramatically deepen your experience of reading the Bible.

For anyone who has worried about the reader-centered nature of the first two steps in this reading method, the turn to form should be a great relief. Although it's not truly the case, paraphrasing and asking how a text makes us feel may seem to suggest that meaning is only a matter of how a reader perceives what she reads. The turn to form in this chapter will demonstrate that those observations and experiences are, in fact, largely determined by the text. While readers play an important role in bringing the text to life, our reading of the text is derived as much from its design as from our own experiences. Thus, to fully comprehend and enjoy what we read, we must do our best to understand how the form of the text enacts those emotions we feel. I have gestured toward the centrality of form in the previous two chapters but have held off on diving into it until now because I wanted to focus on the effects of these poems, to heighten the pleasure of reverse-engineering the causes of those effects. My hope is that understanding the ingenious forms of these two texts we've been examining will complete the joy of reading them.

I want to add one more note on the relation between reader and text with regard to the Bible in particular. It is not only the forms of the Scriptures that generate our experiences with their God-breathed words. The Bible means something to us because, as Walter Brueggemann insists, it "is inherently the live Word of God that addresses us concerning the character and will of the gospel-giving God, empowering us to an alternative life in the world." Brueggemann is struggling here with the authority of the Bible in the everyday lives of Christians. In his struggle with the Scriptures, he goes on to address the complex relationship between reader and text in understanding what we read: "I say 'inherently' because we can affirm that it is in itself intrinsically so. While I give great credence to 'reader response' (how can one not?) and while I believe in the indeterminacy of the text to some large extent, finally the Bible is forceful and consistent in its main theological claim. That claim concerns the conviction that the God who creates the world in love redeems the world in suffering and will consummate the world in joyous well-being."[1] Brueggemann's idea of "inherency" is key, because it reminds us that the Bible itself plays a role in the act of reading, enjoyment, and interpretation. When he references "reader response," Brueggemann is talking about a specific school of literary interpretation that locates the reader, or the reader's larger community, as the ultimate determiner of meaning. Note that his point is to acknowledge that the reader plays a role but to insist on the Bible itself as a consistent source of meaning. He also calls attention to the kind of "indeterminacy" I've frequently mentioned as characteristic of literary texts. Brueggemann understands that biblical texts often resist being reduced to a singular, intellectual idea. At the same time, however, he claims that the Bible makes a "main theological claim." I agree on all counts here. The Bible is the ultimate authority. It drives our interpretation. Individual passages are often indeterminate in the sense of being irreducible to a singular main idea. The Bible, taken as a whole, makes a consistent theological claim. Are some of these statements paradoxical? Yes! Am I comfortable with that? Sometimes! The beautiful thing is that God has given us a word that can both communicate a theological claim and enact a relationship with him. While this book has been focused on the relational dimension of reading, I want to keep in mind that the relationship is possible because the theological claim is true. Let's turn our attention now to *how* texts enact experiences in us through their formal features, practicing on "We Wear the Mask" and then returning to Psalm 119.

Formal Means in "We Wear the Mask"

In chapter 9, I summarized the sense of "We Wear the Mask" by saying that it conveys how African Americans carry a deep pain around with them but mask that pain with a deceptive smile. In chapter 10, I argued that the central emotion of the poem was something like

---

1. Walter Brueggemann, "Biblical Authority: A Personal Reflection," in *Struggling with Scripture*, ed. William Sloane Coffin (Louisville: Westminster John Knox, 2002), 11.

grief-stricken defiance. If we put ourselves in the imaginative world the poem creates and actually position ourselves to feel that emotion, we may very well begin to marvel at how words—dead letters written on paper—can cause us to feel both grieved and defiant. The arrangement of these words is a power similar to that of a song that evokes a feeling in us as we listen. The question that arises now is, How? How can this be possible? How can words do this to/in us? The answer lies, in part, in the form of the words, their relation to one another on the page. We should learn to ask the question like this: Through what formal means does "We Wear the Mask" enact grief-stricken defiance in us? Here's the entire poem once again:

> We wear the mask that grins and lies,
> It hides our cheeks and shades our eyes,—
> This debt we pay to human guile;
> With torn and bleeding hearts we smile,
> And mouth with myriad subtleties.   5
>
> Why should the world be over-wise,
> In counting all our tears and sighs?
> Nay, let them only see us, while
>   We wear the mask.
>
> We smile, but, O great Christ, our cries   10
> To thee from tortured souls arise.
> We sing, but oh the clay is vile
> Beneath our feet, and long the mile;
> But let the world dream otherwise,
>   We wear the mask!   15

There are several formal features we could discuss here, but let's begin with the "tension" between what the speaker of the poem feels and what he shows to the world. This tension is the root cause of the grief and defiance in the poem because the speaker seems prohibited by the world from expressing his pain. The question we should ask is, Through what formal means does Dunbar create this tension?

First and foremost, it is the image of the mask that accomplishes this tension. The mask separates the speaker from the world; it functions as a barrier. We wear masks to conceal our identity by presenting a face to the world that is not our own. Significantly, the mask "hides our cheeks and shades our eyes." It covers the cheeks that would show the tears mentioned later in line 7 and puts the eyes, those windows to the soul, in the shadow. The mask hides the speaker's most expressive features. From the title to the last line of the poem, the mask is central, and thus it makes the idea of a dual identity—what the historian W. E. B. Du Bois would call "double consciousness"—central as well.[2] This duality is what creates the tension between what African American folks experience and what they can show the world, and it is that tension that produces grief and defiance. Consider the brilliance of this image. It embodies that duality perfectly.

But what is imagery, exactly? In the plainest terms, Mary Oliver defines imagery as "the representation of one thing by another thing."[3] Dunbar's image of the mask is straightforward. He helps us understand the experience of duality through an object that splits identity by concealing the true face and presenting a different face to the world. Can you conjure some famous mask wearers? Batman comes to my mind immediately. Bruce Wayne hides his face behind a mask to prevent the world from seeing his true identity. The mask gives him dual personas. He is *both* Bruce Wayne and Batman. These are two distinct identities in one person. Bruce Wayne is *also* Batman just as surely as Batman is *also* Bruce Wayne. The split frequently leads to pain for both Bruce Wayne and Batman. How many times does Bruce want to reveal that he's actually Batman? How many times is the reverse true? Now return to the poem. As James A. Emanuel keenly observes, "Dunbar is careful to show that the mask is grinning, not the black man."[4] The speaker's identity is severed, doubled, split. He seems incapable of removing the mask.

2. W. E. B. Du Bois, *The Souls of Black Folk* (1903; repr., New York: Penguin, 2009), 8. Du Bois defines double consciousness in this famous book as a "two-ness." He argues that every African American experiences an internal division by which they are both "an American, a Negro; two souls, two thoughts, two unreconciled strivings; two warring ideals in one dark body, whose dogged strength alone keeps it from being torn asunder" (8–9).

3. Mary Oliver, *A Poetry Handbook* (New York: Harcourt, Brace, 1994), 92.

4. James A. Emanuel, "Racial Fire in the Poetry of Paul Laurence Dunbar," in *A Singer in the Dawn: Reinterpretations of Paul Laurence Dunbar*, ed. Jay Martin (New York: Dodd, Mead, 1975), 88.

The mask imagery is only the beginning of the formal means through which the poem shapes our reading experience. Take, for instance, the narrative voice. The tension in "We Wear the Mask" comes not only from the mask imagery but also from the choice of a first-person but plural speaker: "*We* wear the mask . . ." Why "we" and not "I"? Why not, "*I* wear the mask . . ."? All but four lines in the poem utilize some form of plural, first-person pronoun, such as "we," "our," or "us." What is the effect of this formal choice? In short, the effect is to create an "us" versus the "world." After all, Dunbar defines the "us" against an outside "world" in lines 6–7 when the speaker wonders, "Why should the world be over-wise, / In counting all our tears and sighs?" The use of a first-person-plural speaker generates an in-group and an out-group, and readers are either in or they're out. Perhaps if, like me, you're not African American, then you find yourself on the outside being offered a brief glimpse into the world of this double consciousness. An African American reader may have a different experience. The poem may function for me as a revelation, whereas it may function for her as a resonance. I may exclaim, "Wow! Is that what it's like?" But she may cry out, "Yes! That's exactly what I've felt." This divergent experience is created through the formal choice of creating the "us" and the "world" through what we call the "voice" of the poem, which, in this case, is a first-person-plural "we." How different it would have been had Dunbar chosen a singular voice, or a third-person voice (as in my paraphrase).

Perhaps you're already seeing why this step in the method is a little more challenging. It requires knowledge not only of poetic form but also of some historical context. For instance, if you don't know about imagery or voice, or if you don't know who W. E. B. Du Bois is or about his concept of double consciousness, you may not be able to do the kind of reading I've just done. Never fear! When it comes to reading the Bible, there is no final exam. The semester, the school year, has no end! What this means practically is that if, for example, you're able to notice that it's the mask that enacts a certain concept or feeling, but you don't know the formal convention of imagery, that's okay. You can understand the poem to a great extent without this technical knowledge, because you're still able to see how Dunbar designed the poem to create the effect you experience when reading it. But I do want to encourage you to dig deeply. When you identify some formal means a text uses to generate a certain reading, do some research. This may mean searching the internet, talking with a pastor, or perhaps investing in a couple good books on literary forms found in the Bible, many of which I've referenced and which you can find in the bibliography at the end. You may also want to consider the next chapter a reference to which you can return to identify common formal features of biblical literature. There's so much more we could say about "We Wear the Mask," but let's turn now to Psalm 119:17–24.

Formal Means in Psalm 119:17–24

First, recall the general sense of the stanza, which I summarized like this: because I am a stranger in an alien and hostile land, I ache for the comfort and direction of God's Word, and when I experience it I am filled with joy and it is as if I am no longer alone but surrounded by wise mentors. The central emotion of these verses is the feeling of having that lonely ache relieved. If you don't feel a deep sense of relief upon reading verse 24, you may not truly understand the poem. But *how* does the verse enact that feeling of relief in us? Through what formal means does it move us? Look again at verse 24:

> Your statutes are my delight;
>   they are my counselors.

The main formal feature at work here is metaphor. A metaphor, quite simply, is the use of a word referring to something familiar to help make something strange or abstract easier to grasp. We use metaphors all the time in speech. I've adapted a simple two-step process from Leland Ryken in which I let the metaphor sink in and interpret it in relation to whatever it represents.[5] In the case of Psalm 119:24, the psalmist calls God's Word his counselors. What is a counselor? Well, usually someone you go to for counsel. Counselors tend to be wise, experienced, honest, and also interested in our well-being. A ruler

5. Leland Ryken, *Words of Delight: A Literary Introduction to the Bible* (Grand Rapids: Baker, 1992), 166–69.

might seek the advice of counselors when facing a tough decision for which the ruler will bear the responsibility. Similarly, I might seek the advice of a counselor when I have to make a decision but know I'm out of my depth.

So far, this probably all makes sense and is not too confusing. We're just letting the literal metaphor sink in. Now we can easily relate it to what it represents—in this case, God's statutes, his Word. The interpretation is straightforward: if I would go to a counselor when facing a tough situation, and if God's Word is my counselor, then I should go to his Word when I am in a tough spot. Hooray! Interpreted. But is that the *meaning* of this passage? Well, if you've followed along from the beginning of the book to this point, then you know that's an incomplete understanding of Psalm 119:24. It's not wrong. It's true and correct that I should seek counsel from God's Word, especially when facing a difficult situation. But that's not total comprehension.

I want to illustrate what it means to comprehend this metaphor with a personal anecdote. A few years ago during an especially stressful semester I had a student come to me with a difficult problem. I had no idea what to do or how to respond. I felt inadequate, even fearful. We scheduled a time to meet to discuss the matter, but I was plagued by worry and doubt in the days leading up to the meeting. As I prayed over the matter one morning, I was reading along in Psalm 119 when I came to verse 24. Immediately I was struck with what I needed to do: I needed to seek counsel. And so, I thought to myself, I know, I'll go see Dr. Hammett. John Hammett is one of my senior colleagues. He is older, wiser, and way more experienced, and I knew he had faced almost every student problem imaginable. I thought to myself, I should go see him; he'll know what to do. A sense of relief, assurance, even confidence washed over me. I met with Dr. Hammett and, sure enough, he prayed for me and gave me wise counsel. Though it was still difficult, I went into my meeting with the student with a sense of peace and came out thankful to Dr. Hammett and to the psalmist.

I went back to Psalm 119:24 after the meeting and reread the verse over and over again. I had the revelation that understanding God's Word as my counselor meant more than giving mental assent to the fact that I should seek wisdom from his Word. I knew this already. But now I understood that his Word was intended to enact that sense of relief, assurance, even confidence in me. I wanted to read his Word and sit across from it as badly as I wanted to meet with my wise colleague. I not only knew the Bible contained wisdom; I actually felt relief when reading, to the point that I wanted to read it more, to the point that the next time I faced a difficult situation, I immediately, preconsciously desired to encounter God in his Word. But the key thing to note here is that I likely would not have had this experience/understanding of the text had the psalmist simply said, "God's Word provides counsel." The form of the poem accomplished this love for the Bible in me. It was the use of the metaphor, the personification of God's Word as a counsel*or*, that enacted that sense of relief and stoked a longing for communion with the Scriptures.

In the next chapter, I spend a little more time on common formal features of biblical literature in an effort to help build your knowledge and so bolster your understanding of and delight in God's Word. I also discuss further how form grounds our reading in history.

EXERCISE 11
Formal Means

1. Read Psalm 119:25–32.
2. Write a few sentences pinpointing what specific part/feature in the poem seems to engender the emotion you identified in exercise 10.
3. Reflect on how the text enacts this sense and emotion in you.
4. Pray that God would deepen your understanding of the verses.

CHAPTER TWELVE

A Short Compendium of Forms

Form grounds our reading in history. Metaphor and meter, rhyme and rhythm—these formal conventions of literature have distinct histories, uses, and effects. For example, if I want to understand how metaphor produces meaning in a Bible verse, it helps to know how metaphor functioned in the historical and cultural context in which the verse was written, as well as how it works in my own language today. When we begin to examine how a literary text enacts emotion and conveys ideas through its formal design, we are necessarily grounding our reading in the histories of the text and the reader. As I suggested in the last chapter, however, the historicity and technical nature of form require a specialized body of knowledge. My purpose in carrying our reading method all the way through to form is not to suggest that you must be a professional literary critic or Bible scholar to understand the Scriptures. Remember, you can be moved by a metaphor without understanding exactly what a metaphor is and how it works. But a little bit of formal knowledge can deepen your understanding of and pleasure in reading the text. Not only does it enable you to appreciate how the text has moved and informed you, but it also expands your knowledge of the text's history and context and your own as well. For the nonspecialist, I recommend William Logan's pronouncement for literary critics writing for broad audiences: "You have to understand the mechanics, but you don't need to go on about it."[1] Likewise, I would say to the reader who wants to maximize her experience reading the Bible, it's important to understand form, but you don't need to obsess over it like an academic.

In the last three chapters, we read "We Wear the Mask" and Psalm 119:17–24 by working our way through their general sense, central emotion, and some formal features. Replicating steps 1 and 2 on your own will be fairly simple, but tackling step 3 will be more difficult without some command of literary forms. Although I provided some explanation and examples of imagery and metaphor, many readers will likely benefit from short overviews of some of the more common formal features of literature they will encounter in the Bible. This chapter offers such an overview. Beginning with parallelism, the foundation of biblical poetry, I offer introductory descriptions and brief examples of various elements of form you will find when reading both literary and nonliterary passages in the Bible. After all, much of the more informational prose in the Scriptures utilizes poetic language. This catalog of forms is not meant to be exhaustive, but if you familiarize yourself with what you find here, you will be better equipped to identify and research other formal features on your own.

Parallelism

The explanation of parallelism will be the longest and most technical of the explanations in this chapter, because this convention is so fundamental to biblical literature. Tremper Longman defines parallelism as "the correspondence which occurs between the phrases of a poetic line."[2] Parallelism is the most common poetic form in the Bible; we could even point out instances of parallelism included in passages not considered to be poetry. So when I use the term *poetic*, I'm not only

---

1. William Logan, "Against Aesthetics," *New Criterion* 32, no. 1 (September 2013): 21.
2. Tremper Longman III, *How to Read the Psalms* (Downers Grove, IL: Inter-Varsity, 1988), 95.

referring to texts that are poetry; I'm referring to a particular use of language. There is perhaps no greater expert on parallelism than the biblical scholar Adele Berlin. Offering an even broader definition than Longman, Berlin argues that parallelism "is a correspondence of one thing with another."[3] In other words, parallelism is a use of language that puts two things in relation to one another. "The nature of the correspondence varies," Berlin explains, "but in general it involves repetition or the substitution of things which are equivalent on one or more linguistic levels."[4] For instance, in the first two lines of Psalm 24, David uses parallelism to say the same thing twice:

> The earth is the LORD's, and everything in it,
> the world, and all who live in it;

If the earth and everything in it is the Lord's, as we learn in the first line, then that includes "the world, and all who live in it," as we're told in the second line. In this example of parallelism, the idea in line 1 is repeated in line 2 in a slightly different way to show comprehensiveness.

However, it's important to note that "equivalence" means sameness but not identity. For instance, hot and cold are equivalent in a way that hot and noisy are not. Even though hot and cold are obviously opposites, they are related. They are equivalent in the sense that they both describe the same general concept, temperature. Consider verse 4 of Psalm 24. After asking "Who may ascend the mountain of the LORD? / Who may stand in his holy place?" in verse 3, David answers his own question:

> The one who *has* clean hands and a pure heart,
> who *does not* trust in an idol
> or swear by a false god.

The positive and negative answers in the first and second lines characterize a similar person. The one who can ascend God's mountain and stand in his holy place is the one who *does* have clean hands and

---

3. Adele Berlin, *The Dynamics of Biblical Parallelism*, rev. ed. (Grand Rapids: Eerdmans, 2008; first published 1985 by Indiana University Press [Bloomington]), 2.
4. Berlin, *Dynamics of Biblical Parallelism*, 2.

a pure heart but also the one who *does not* trust in an idol. The parallelism here uses corresponding positive and negative descriptions. Those who can stand with God have the purity of clean hands, not the impurity of idol worship. Equivalence may refer to two different versions of the same thing, as in Psalm 24:1, or an opposition between two equivalent things, as in Psalm 24:4.

But how does parallelism shape our reading of the larger texts? To answer this question, I want to work through an example offered by Berlin from the book of Judges. The story of Jael and Sisera is told twice in this book, once in prose and once in poetry. Berlin examines the similarities and differences between the two versions to demonstrate how parallelism causes us to pay attention to different things in the poetic telling than those we might notice in the prose story. Both versions use parallelism, but to different effects. When Sisera comes to Jael in the prose rendering of Judges 4:19 and asks for a drink, the writer uses parallelism by repeating the language for the action of drinking:

> He said to her, "Please give me a little drink of water, for I am thirsty." And she opened the milk container and gave him a drink, and covered him.

According to Berlin, the repetition of "give/gave me/him a drink" does not do much to play up the correspondence between water and milk. However, in the poetry passage, "the contrast between *water* and *milk* is unmistakable because the clauses in which they occur are exactly parallel syntactically (even in the order of the components), and there is an inherent semantic contrast":

> Water he asked,
> Milk she gave;
> In a princely bowl she offered curds.

What I want to emphasize is Berlin's claim that "this forces the contrast between *water* and *milk* into the mind of the reader."[5] In other

---

5. Berlin, *Dynamics of Biblical Parallelism*, 12. The translations from the Hebrew here are Berlin's as well.

words, the form of the language focuses our attention, shapes our reading, determines our interpretation differently in the poetry version than in the prose version. We know that the poetry passage could have a different effect because we have another version with which we can compare it.

You will find many different forms of parallelism throughout the Bible, sometimes creating comparison, other times contrast, sometimes clarifying an idea or emotion, other times creating ambiguity. The natural question you should ask when identifying parallelism as integral to the way a passage moves you is, Why create this equivalence? Why focus on the opposition between water and milk in the poetic retelling of Jael and Sisera's story? What is the effect? Berlin, and the scholars she cites, argue that the stark contrast between water and milk in the poetry version breaks up the narrative flow of the story, or what she calls the "stringlike quality" of the account. The poem, Berlin argues, is more nonlinear than the prose: "Now the same sequence is present in the poetic account . . . —but the stringlike quality is gone."[6] This is a great observation because it teaches us to push our interpretation as far as possible by asking, What is the effect of a more nonlinear version? Or we might ask, What does the nonlinear account give us that the linear account does not, and vice versa? Keep asking until you feel like you can't ask even once more . . . and then ask just once more.

Whether the equivalence produces emphasis, contrast, clarity, or ambiguity, you can always continue to question why that form would be utilized to produce that effect. Keep in mind that the ultimate goal is not to resolve everything or answer every question but to extend your pursuit of God in his Word.

Imagery

In the last chapter we talked about Dunbar's use of imagery in "We Wear the Mask" and the psalmist's use of metaphor and personification in his representation of God's statutes as counselors. *Metaphor*

6. Berlin, *Dynamics of Biblical Parallelism*, 14.

and *personification*, along with *simile*, are forms of imagery. You may recall Mary Oliver's simple, yet profound, definition of imagery: "the representation of one thing by another thing." She follows this definition with an example: "A statue is an image."[7] The statue is not whatever/whomever it represents. The statue is a thing that represents another thing. So too, in language, writers use images to help readers see what they are imagining. John Sutherland calls images "pictures in the head."[8] Anytime you run across an image, you should pause to consider these questions:

1. What is the image itself?
2. What is it being used to represent?
3. What is the effect of representing that thing by an image rather than describing the thing itself?

These simple questions will keep you tethered to the reality that form shapes understanding in a special way in literary writing. Here are brief explanations of the basic forms of imagery.

Simile

A simile is a kind of image that compares one thing to another by describing it as being "like" or "as" the other thing. You may recall the opening lines from Frances Ellen Watkins Harper's poem "Eliza Harris," which we read in chapter 8: "Like a fawn from the arrow, startled and wild, / A woman swept by us, bearing a child." We can see that the fawn is an image because, as Oliver says, one thing is represented as another thing—a woman as a young deer. We know it is a simile because she uses an explicit comparison, signaled by the word "like," to accomplish the representation. This comparison should be familiar to readers of the Bible, who will recall these lines of Psalm 42:1: "As the deer pants for streams of water, / so my soul pants for you, my God." My soul thirsts for God just "as" a deer

---

7. Mary Oliver, *A Poetry Handbook* (New York: Harcourt, Brace, 1994), 92.
8. John Sutherland, *How Literature Works: 50 Key Concepts* (New York: Oxford University Press, 2011), 96.

thirsts for water. Jesus uses similes all the time in his attempts to help us understand the kingdom of heaven. Consider these examples from Matthew 13: "The kingdom of heaven is like a man who sowed good seed" (v. 24). "The kingdom of heaven is like a mustard seed" (v. 31). "The kingdom of heaven is like treasure hidden in a field" (v. 44). "The kingdom of heaven is like a merchant looking for fine pearls" (v. 45).

Metaphor

A metaphor is a kind of image that compares one thing to another but without using the explicit language of "like" or "as" the way a simile does. The point, as with all imagery, is to create a connection between two things we might not normally associate with one another to help us see/understand the idea, thing, or feeling the writer is representing in the text. In metaphor the writer simply makes the comparison implicitly: "The LORD is my strength and my shield" (Ps. 28:7). Of course, God is not a shield. David calls God a shield as a way of understanding what it's like to be protected by God.

Metonymy

Metonymy is a kind of imagery that substitutes one thing, idea, or person for something related to it. For example, a journalist might report that "the White House said today that a new poet laureate will be named next week." Of course, the White House is a building made of wood, stone, plaster, and metal; it cannot speak. It is a metonym for the president of the United States, his office, his staff, his agenda. Consider how "heaven" is often used metonymically throughout the Scriptures as a stand-in for God. Jesus asks the Jewish leaders if John's baptism was "from heaven, or of human origin" in Matthew 21. "Heaven" here is a metonym for God.

Synecdoche

Synecdoche is a kind of imagery that substitutes a part of a thing for the whole thing. Sharon Hamilton offers the example of a fleet of ships described as "forty sails" and reminds us of the biblical phrase "daily bread" as a synecdoche for "the food needed for sustenance."[9] Michael Travers calls our attention to synecdoche in Psalm 45: "In your majesty ride forth victoriously / in the cause of truth, humility and justice; / let your right hand achieve awesome deeds." Here "your right hand" is a synecdoche for God and his great power.[10]

Ambiguity

Ambiguity may seem like a liability, but it is vital to literary language. Terry Eagleton makes an important distinction between ambiguity and ambivalence: "Ambivalence happens when we have two meanings, both of which are determinate but which differ from one another. Ambiguity happens when two or more senses of a word merge into each other to the point where the meaning itself becomes indeterminate."[11] Some passages of Scripture may be designed to leave us without a clear resolution. Consider the ambiguity surrounding the thorn in Paul's side. While Paul uses his affliction to teach us about faithfulness, he never discloses exactly what the thorn is. Sometimes things are ambiguous not because we fail to understand but because they were designed to remain unresolved. The biblical scholar Paul Raabe outlines four types of ambiguity in the Psalms alone, concluding that ambiguity in the Psalms is often employed not evasively or deceitfully but to amuse us and hold our attention. It is also evidence of the psalmists' mastery of language and the joy they took in writing. "But," he continues, "even more important, such multivalence functions to engage the hearers/readers, to cause them to interact with the psalm, and to lead them to recognize the truth of the various possible interpretations."[12] I include this formal feature not to suggest that all difficult passages are purposefully ambiguous but to encourage us to wrestle with passages that seem resistant to singular interpretations.

9. Sharon Hamilton, *Essential Literary Terms: A Brief Norton Guide with Exercises* (New York: Norton, 2007), 41.

10. Michael E. Travers, *Encountering God in the Psalms* (Grand Rapids: Kregel, 2003), 41.

11. Terry Eagleton, *How to Read a Poem* (Malden, MA: Blackwell, 2007), 125.

12. Paul R. Raabe, "Deliberate Ambiguity in the Psalter," *Journal of Biblical Literature* 110, no. 2 (Summer 1991): 227.

It may just be that they were designed to draw us in. It may just be that they were written to keep us in the text.

Narrative versus Story

The distinction between narrative and story is relevant to any biblical writing that lays out a series of related events. Whether the passage is historical or parable, in reading any tale we must distinguish between what happens (story) and the way it is told (narrative). Consider the example of Judges 4 and 5 given earlier in this chapter. The same events (story) are told in two different ways (narrative). The story is the events that play out and the entities involved. The narrative is the representation of the story. To understand the Bible, we must recognize that our access to its story (events and entities) is always mediated by its narrative (how those events and entities get represented). In other words, we come to the story through the narrative. Consider the three Synoptic Gospels, Matthew, Mark, and Luke. In these Gospels, many of the same stories are told, but sometimes they are represented differently. From a literary perspective, the point is not to note inconsistencies but to attend to what the differences in narrative representation can teach us about the stories being told.

Direct Discourse

Any time you see quotation marks show up in a poem or a story, you are reading direct discourse. Take, for instance, Psalm 31:22:

> In my alarm I said,
>   "I am cut off from your sight!"
> Yet you heard my cry for mercy
>   when I called to you for help.

The sentence "I am cut off from your sight!" appears in quotation marks, signaling that someone is speaking. In the English language, we use quotation marks to signal direct discourse and thus to distinguish the voice that is speaking from the narrator or speaker of the story/poem, even when the voice and the narrator are the same person as in this case. In this example, David is the narrator/speaker of the poem, but he no longer feels cut off from God's sight as he did in the moment he memorializes in the poem.

No Meaning without Form

This brief compendium of forms is a snapshot of just some of the many literary forms found in the Scriptures, though it should be enough to get you started as you begin to consider how the form of the text shapes your understanding. My goal here is not to provide an exhaustive catalog of the full range of poetic forms found in Scripture. You can find excellent books that do this. I recommend Tremper Longman's *How to Read the Psalms* and Robert Alter's *The Art of Biblical Poetry* as accessible introductions; Leland Ryken's *Words of Delight* as a still-accessible, yet more textbook-like read; and Adele Berlin's *The Dynamics of Biblical Parallelism* or F. W. Dobbs-Allsopp's *On Biblical Poetry* for those interested in more technical examinations of the dominant poetic forms in the Bible.[13] On conceptualizing the importance of formal features to meaning in the Bible, Ryken says quite simply that "the poets who wrote the poetry of the Bible regarded these things as important. So should we."[14] For the writers of the Bible, the form of the writing was essential.

Form, then, is integral to meaning. Whatever passage of Scripture you're reading would not mean the same thing if the writer had chosen a different metaphor or had chosen to use a different trope altogether. The formal features are not interchangeable decorations; they are essential. Form makes meaning.

13. Tremper Longman III, *How to Read the Psalms* (Downers Grove, IL: Inter-Varsity, 1988); Robert Alter, *The Art of Biblical Poetry*, rev. ed. (New York: Basic Books, 2011); Leland Ryken, *Words of Delight: A Literary Introduction to the Bible* (Grand Rapids: Baker, 1992); Adele Berlin, *The Dynamics of Biblical Parallelism*, rev. ed. (Grand Rapids: Eerdmans, 2008; first published 1985 by Indiana University Press [Bloomington]); F. W. Dobbs-Allsopp, *On Biblical Poetry* (New York: Oxford University Press, 2015).
14. Ryken, *Words of Delight*, 211.

Conclusion

Negative Capability and Habituation

I began this book with a diagnosis, a theory that most readers of the Bible have been trained to read it primarily for information. Our eyes have become accustomed to a certain kind of light, one that makes facts, instructions, and practical applications easy to see but leaves emotion in the shadows. I called this mode of reading a "hermeneutics of information." But there was a second part of the diagnosis: not only is there a problem with *how* we read the Bible, but there is also a problem with *what* we think the Bible is. If we tend to read it for instruction, then the book itself becomes an instruction manual. This view creates problems whenever we encounter passages that are designed to do more than simply convey information. One problem is that it can create frustrations with the text. We may avoid Scriptures that don't offer what we take to be clear instruction or doctrinal claims. But another problem is that it can lead us to misread those passages by motivating us to reduce them to propositions. In other words, a hermeneutics of information can encourage misunderstanding by leading us to look for singularity when a text offers complexity.

Retraining ourselves as readers requires becoming more comfortable with meaning as a complex phenomenon made up of ideas and emotions. The early nineteenth-century British poet John Keats coined the term *negative capability* to describe the ability to wrestle with and rest in uncertainty. I believe this is a quality both of good literature and of good reading. In other words, good works of literature leave room for us to grapple with uncertainty, and good readers are capable of living in that uncertainty without always needing to resolve it into a clear and final message. Negative capability has very specific connotations when it comes to reading the Bible. I would argue that where we encounter and experience uncertainty, or multiplicity, in God's Word, we are being invited to speculate, question, and wonder. Our own negative capability is the ability to pursue God without a definite end in sight. We learn to pursue God in the Scriptures for God's own sake. In the first part of the conclusion below, I examine this idea of negative capability and its relation to the Bible. In the second part, I explore Aristotle's idea of habituation in an effort to prepare us for what it will be like to become different kinds of readers. After all, it's taken you your entire lifetime to become the kind of reader you are now, so it stands to reason that retraining yourself will take some time and effort. A little disclaimer can go a long way in cultivating realistic expectations.

Negative Capability

In a famous letter to his brothers, John Keats praises Shakespeare for how his work possesses and produces "negative capability." Keats defines "negative capability" as the capability of "being in uncertainties, Mysteries, doubts, without any irritable reaching after fact & reason."[1] He's just finished contrasting a famous painting by Benjamin West entitled *Death on the Pale Horse* with Shakespeare's play *King Lear*. What makes Shakespeare superior to West, in Keats's estimation, is that *King Lear* presents the complexities of human experience without resolving them into a neat and tidy moral or explanation. West's painting, while masterful and accomplished, lacks intensity; it fails to provoke, or enact, speculation. It's more answer

---

1. John Keats, "A Letter to George and Thomas Keats," in *The Critical Tradition: Classic Texts and Contemporary Trends*, ed. David H. Richter (New York: St. Martin's Press, 1989), 320.

than question. For Keats, the most beautiful and true works of art and literature are those that move our imaginations because they resist easy explanations.

Perhaps we humans find such works to be beautiful because they resonate with the complexities of our own experiences and to be frustrating because we long for those complexities to be resolved. But human life, like the Bible, is filled with paradoxes. We know what it's like to be happy and sad at the same time, to both love and hate someone, to find pleasure in pain. The Bible tells us that "whoever finds their life will lose it, and whoever loses their life for my sake will find it" (Matt. 10:39). It tells us that the poor are rich and the rich are poor (James 1:9–10). It insists that the more we please ourselves, the less satisfied we'll be (Prov. 27:20). Everyone knows that the first shall be last and the last shall be first (Matt. 19:30). How can weakness be strength and strength weakness (2 Cor. 12:9–10)? The worst thing we could do would be to try to reduce these paradoxes to simple imperatives: lose your life; be poor; don't please yourself; be last; be weak. What would it even mean to be weak? These important teachings are irreducible to singular takeaways. Instead, they encourage us to meditate on the order of things as we understand it and the order of things as God understands it. The two are often at odds, and if his ways are higher than ours (Isa. 55:8–9), there is at least some sense in which we cannot fully understand these things in our human finitude.

Keats's idea of negative capability is important here because he represents it both as a quality of the work itself and of the reader of the work. In other words, works of art and literature that leave room for further speculation and consideration are superior to those that don't, because of their negative capability, and readers who are able to make peace with "uncertainties, Mysteries, doubts, without any irritable reaching after fact & reason" are better readers because they possess negative capability.

Now, this doesn't mean that biblical passages with a lot of negative capability are superior to passages that are more prescriptive, historical, or theological-philosophical. Literary Scriptures are not somehow more inspired, authoritative, or sufficient than nonliterary Scriptures. They may be more aesthetically pleasing at times, but keep in mind that aesthetic pleasure does not have the same priority in all forms of writing. While it will not be absent from a Pauline epistle or historical account, in those genres artistry may not be a primary goal. We must simply ask ourselves what a particular text is trying to accomplish, what it's *for*.

But what the concept of negative capability does mean for our reading of the Scriptures is that we can learn to recognize and read differently those literary texts designed to incite our imaginations and encourage contemplation. God is not only inviting us to study his Word in order to know right from wrong; he desires a relationship with us. The Scriptures offer texts designed to accomplish both. The literary portions of the Bible, those that present and engender negative capability, want to grab and hold your attention. They don't want you to look for the quick fact or reason; they want you to question, wonder, struggle, rejoice in your efforts to know God. To return a final time to Matthew Zapruder, he defines negative capability for the reader as a state in which "you can accept a succession of things, especially if they contradict each other, in order to allow within yourself an experience that you will not have elsewhere in life."[2] To suspend our desire to resolve the seeming contradiction between being first and being last is to dwell in the mystery of God's ways, which are so different from ours. To accept for a moment that winners lose and losers win (Mark 8:36; Phil. 3:8) is to allow ourselves to experience God. Such acceptance, contemplation, and wonder are part of why there are poems in the Bible. God wants to commune with us, and communion is harder to achieve if we are simply consulting a handbook or instruction manual.

Reflect for just a minute on your relationship with a person you love, perhaps a spouse, child, grandchild, friend, sibling, cousin, parent, or grandparent. What does this relationship look like? When you spend time together, what do you do, think, say? Are there subjects to which you return in your conversations again and again? Must you be talking whenever you're together? Do you ever just sit together? How about you and God? What does your relationship look like? What do you talk about? Do you ever just sit together? There are passages of Scripture and ways of reading that encourage us to meditate on

---

2. Matthew Zapruder, *Why Poetry* (New York: Ecco, 2017), 105.

God, to commune with him personally, and, sometimes, just to sit with him. Oftentimes, these texts are the kinds that raise more questions than answers, the kinds that resist easy conclusions, the literary kinds: poems, parables, stories, and poetic passages of informational prose. The more uncertain, mysterious, or doubtful the text, the more chance we have for the kind of communion with God that draws us closer to him through time spent in meditation and wonder. Keats says the best readers are those who are capable of "being in" such uncertainties "without any irritable reaching after fact & reason." I would say "being in" such uncertainties when reading the Bible can lead to a love for the text itself and for the God at its center.

The literary passages designed to appeal to our hearts have a lot to teach us, though the kind of knowledge may not simply be the stuff of history, theology, philosophy, or ethics. It is a kind of emotional and relational knowledge, a love for God that can revolutionize our understanding of the history, theology, philosophy, and ethics we find in the Bible, including its literary portions. In short, you can't understand the Bible if you don't love it. To love it, you must learn how to read it. To learn how to read it, you must know what kind of thing it is. To know what kind of thing it is, you need to be able to distinguish between the different forms it contains. This book has been dedicated to teaching you how to identify and read the literary forms in the Bible, especially the poetry. If you are now better equipped to read the Bible, perhaps you also have a better sense of what kind of thing it is. It is not only an instruction manual but also a work of art made for our pleasure and communion with God. If you can approach it as a work of art, then you're learning how to read it like one. The more you read it as a work of literary art, the more you'll come to love it. And the more you love God's Word, the more you'll keep it. Keeping it is what it means to love God, as Jesus tells his disciples in John 14:21.

Habituation

There is no magic trick or shortcut I can offer in developing this love for God via his Word. In his famous book on ethics, Aristotle argues that our state of being, or our character, "results from the repetition of similar activities."[3] Thus, humans experience both states and actions. The main difference between the two is that we cannot immediately control our state, or character. In other words, if you're not the kind of person who gets up early every morning to commune with God in his Word, then you cannot simply decide to become such a person and, voilà, now you're that person. However, in a strange twist, it turns out that we develop our states, or characters, willingly by "the repetition of similar activities." In other words, we form our character through our repeated actions. So here's the key: while you cannot instantly change your character, you can instantly change an individual action. For example, while you cannot become overnight the kind of person who gets up and reads the Bible every morning, you can choose to do so tomorrow. If you continue to choose this action for long enough, Aristotle argues, through habituation you can change your state, or character. You can become the kind of person who gets up early to commune with God every day. This habituation will take time, but you can change your character via your actions.

Why am I talking about Aristotle, habituation, and changing your character? Well, because I know that if you've taken this book seriously and want to love the Scriptures, then you're going to want to be the kind of person who loves the Scriptures right away. But I also know that you cannot change who you are in a single day, or even a week, or maybe even a month. I do know, though, that through the repetition of the kind of reading we've explored in these chapters, you can become the kind of person who loves the Scriptures and communes with God through them regularly. It's going to take time, practice, and patience. But remember, it's not a race. There is no deadline. The journey itself is the goal in this case. The process is *how* you grow closer to God. Every individual action is a choice to fellowship with him.

If the language of habituation is too philosophical or too irreligious for you, then you'll find comfort in knowing that Christians have had their own understanding and practice of habit for centuries.

3. Aristotle, *Nicomachean Ethics*, trans. Terence Irwin, 2nd ed. (Indianapolis: Hackett, 1999), 19.

Perhaps you'd be more comfortable with language like Richard J. Foster's "spiritual discipline" or James K. A. Smith's "liturgy." As a Baptist, I didn't grow up with words like *liturgy* and had never heard of many "high church" practices. I wasn't taught to think of the Lord's Supper as a sacrament or of the various parts of the worship service as rituals. If I had encountered a book about liturgies in high school, I would have been suspicious. So when I first read Foster's *Celebration of Discipline* in college, I was challenged but not thrown off because Foster doesn't use "high church" language often. He talks about the power of "ingrained habits," but emphasizes spiritual disciplines such as meditation, fasting, simplicity, and confession as good habits designed to invite the Holy Spirit into our lives to do the work only the Spirit can do.[4] If you're a Protestant in a tradition that doesn't emphasize ritual, sacrament, or readings from texts like *The Book of Common Prayer*, then Foster's book may be a good introduction to the idea of spiritual disciplines as habit.

A liturgy is a form of religious worship, and so when someone talks about liturgies, they are usually talking about a practice or habit of worship in the church. But what James K. A. Smith argues is that our entire lives are filled with liturgies, not just our time at church. We are active participants in what he calls "cultural liturgies," habits and practices that form our desires but which we do not always recognize as such because we experience them outside the walls of the church. What's important about a liturgy of any kind is that it involves our bodies. Whether we are raising the communion cup to our mouths or swiping our credit cards, "liturgies aim our love to different ends precisely by training our hearts through our bodies."[5] Even the most mundane actions can be liturgical. In her book *Liturgy of the Ordinary*, Tish Harrison Warren offers accounts of making our beds, brushing our teeth, and sitting in traffic as habits with the capacity to form us spiritually.[6]

4. Richard J. Foster, *Celebration of Discipline: The Path to Spiritual Growth*, rev. ed. (Downers Grove, IL: InterVarsity, 1988), 4–6.

5. James K. A. Smith, *Desiring the Kingdom: Worship, Worldview, and Cultural Formation*, Cultural Liturgies 1 (Grand Rapids: Baker Academic, 2009), 25.

6. Tish Harrison Warren, *Liturgy of the Ordinary: Sacred Practices in Everyday Life* (Downers Grove, IL: InterVarsity, 2016).

The point is that the actions we take are all significant, but the actions we repeat every day are especially important because they make us who we are. Aristotle saw these daily actions as habits that form our character, and he was right. But they are so much more than that. We are not mere brains nor are we mere bodies. We are breath and strength, heart and head, soul and spirit. We are resolutely spiritual creatures, made in God's image to worship him. Our most habitual actions are spiritual disciplines, liturgies whose cumulative effect is to tell us what/who we really worship. My prayer for readers of this book is that you would recognize your reading of the Bible as, itself, a spiritual act, a liturgy. Whenever you do it, you are forming yourself as a worshiper of God as well as forming your relationship with him. If we recognize the very act of reading as spiritual, then perhaps we may realize how vital it is in our efforts to love God. Here we have his very words in our hands! Do we love them? Do you love the Scriptures? I hope that this book has cultivated in you a new way of seeing and relating to the Bible. If you put its principles and suggestions into practice with good faith and a desire for communion with God, I believe you will be transformed into the kind of person who loves his Word.

Reading Practices

What follows is a selection of models for reading practice that you might try on different days to set in motion the actions that will change your reading character. You will need fifteen minutes of uninterrupted quiet to complete these reading practices, so set yourself up in a place and at a time where this will be possible. If you're in a noisy environment or easily subject to interruption, you won't complete the practice and may get frustrated or feel like you've failed. Set yourself up for success. You can repeat the same practice with the same passages or swap out the passages as you become accustomed to reading this way. Also, feel free to expand the time. I find that when I'm struggling, fifteen minutes is plenty. On days when things come a bit more easily, I will spend as much time as I'm able. I recommend getting a notebook to dedicate to this practice. It doesn't have to be expensive or fancy, just something in which you can collect your reflections and meditations.

READING PRACTICE 1
The LORD Is My Shepherd; I Shall Not Want

1. Read Psalm 23:1. Read the entire psalm if you like, but come back to verse 1 and read it over a few times.
2. Write verse 1 out, copying it directly from your Bible.
3. Write a few different versions of it in your own words. Experiment with different metaphors for God that function similarly to "shepherd" in your mind. What people/positions operate as shepherds in your life? What does it mean to declare that you "shall not want"?
4. Spend any remaining time sitting in silence with your eyes closed, thinking about the implications of God as our shepherd.

READING PRACTICE 2
Now You Are the Body of Christ

1. Read 1 Corinthians 12:12–31.
2. Write out a list of other similes Paul could have used instead of a body to describe the church.
3. What is the effect of using "body" as opposed to one of these other possibilities?
4. Spend any remaining time sitting in silence, reflecting on the local body to which you belong and how it compares to Paul's poetic representation of the church.

READING PRACTICE 3
Chasing after the Wind

1. Read Ecclesiastes 2:10–11.
2. In the margin of the passage, write the central emotion of the verses in a single word or short phrase.
3. Examine the verses closely to determine how the passage enacts that emotion in you. Have you ever worked hard at something only to feel that it was pointless? Try to think of a specific example from your life to help you relate to the verses.
4. Spend any remaining time meditating on that image of chasing after the wind.

READING PRACTICE 4
In the Beginning

1. Read Genesis 1:1 and John 1:1.
2. Write out at least one phrase that functions similarly to "in the beginning" (for example, "once upon a time").
3. Reflect on how these phrases operate and what they communicate to readers.
4. Meditate on why John would invoke Genesis 1:1 at the beginning of his Gospel.

READING PRACTICE 5
A Man Was Going

1. Read Luke 10:25–37.
2. Reread verses 25–29 a few times and consider the fact that verses 30–35 are the answer to the question asked in verse 29.
3. Write out why you believe Jesus responded to this expert in the law with a story rather than with a direct answer. Does Jesus answer his question? What is the answer?
4. Meditate on the difference between a direct answer and a parable.

READING PRACTICE 6
Slaves of God

1. Read Romans 6:15–23.
2. Slavery took a different form in Paul's time than the form most modern Westerners imagine when they hear the term. But in any case, a slave is someone without absolute freedom. Write out a few other paradoxes Paul could have used to express the basic idea of this passage. For example, if to be a slave is to be a free person, then perhaps we could say that to be a student is to be a teacher.
3. Reflect on the effect of this paradox on your attempts to understand sin and righteousness as Paul describes them in this passage.
4. Sit in silence for a few minutes and consider what it would mean to be a slave to righteousness and how that would accomplish freedom.

READING PRACTICE 7
I Am Laid Low in the Dust

1. Sit in silence for five minutes and reflect on a time in which you felt defeated.
2. Read Psalm 119:25. Read the remainder of the stanza (vv. 26–32).
3. What is the central emotion of this stanza? Write out a few good emotion words in the margin of your Bible.
4. Ask God to make you into a person who longs for his Word in both good and bad times.

Afterword

Reading Aloud

Today there is nothing strange about reading silently. But when Saint Augustine saw Saint Ambrose reading silently to himself in Milan in AD 384, it was odd enough that he remarked on it in his autobiographical *Confessions*: "When he read, his eyes travelled across the page and his heart sought into the sense, but voice and tongue were silent. No one was forbidden to approach him nor was it his custom to require that visitors should be announced: but when we came in to him we often saw him reading and always to himself; and after we had sat long in silence, unwilling to interrupt a work on which he was so intent, we would depart again."[1] I find this account comical, the thought of Augustine and other young scholars and acolytes coming up to this revered teacher only to find him preoccupied, waiting for a while to see if he would acknowledge them, and then leaving as if they hadn't come there to seek him out. The novelty of reading silently seems to have flustered them. Was Saint Ambrose praying? Was he meditating on the text in hand? Not entirely sure of what was happening, and not wanting to be a nuisance, they would leave him in silence without ever having said a word.

1. Augustine, *Confessions*, 2nd ed., trans. F. J. Sheed (Indianapolis: Hackett, 2006), book 6, chap. 3, p. 98.

What's important about this story for our purposes is the strangeness
of reading silently. In his book *A History of Reading*, Alberto Manguel
claims that "Augustine's description of Ambrose's silent reading (including the remark that he *never* read aloud) is the first definite instance
recorded in Western literature."[2] There was a time when reading aloud
was the rule and reading silently the exception. From Augustine's time
through the Middle Ages, a transformation in reading practices took
place. We became primarily silent readers. Writers and scribes stopped
jamming words together on their scrolls, codices, and pages; they sys-
tematized punctuation; they invented paragraphs; all of this, in part, to
facilitate silent reading.[3] While Scripture may be read aloud at church,
or we might read a funny text message to a friend, Augustine would
have no cause to remark on Ambrose's silent reading were he to find
the famous teacher sitting quietly with a book today. Just the opposite
is true: if Augustine were living in our society today and he walked in
on a spiritual mentor reading aloud alone in his study, he might find
such behavior odd and worthy of memorializing in his autobiography.

I believe we need to resurrect the practice of reading aloud, especially with the Scriptures. My purpose here is not to discourage silent
reading. There is something intimate and meditative about taking
the Scriptures in with noiseless devotion. However, there are three
reasons why we need to read aloud. The first is that reading aloud
forces us to slow down. The second is that the sound and sense of
the words aid in our understanding. The third is that reading aloud
also lends itself to reading in community.

Slowing Down

Before considering reading aloud as a strategy for slowing down, let's
notice the somewhat counterintuitive nature of reading aloud. Ironi-
cally, the easiest setting in which to read aloud is solitude. Though I

2. Alberto Manguel, *A History of Reading* (New York: Viking, 1996), 43. Recall
that in Sheed's translation of Augustine, which I cited above, the phrase "for he never
read aloud," noted by Manguel, is translated "we often saw him reading and *always
to himself*" (*Confessions*, 98; emphasis added).
3. The history of silent reading in this paragraph comes from Manguel, *History
of Reading*, 48–49.

will talk about the communal benefits to reading aloud in a moment, I want to encourage us to read the Scriptures aloud when we are alone, perhaps particularly when we are alone. If you aim to cultivate the kind of reading practice I've outlined in the preceding pages, reading aloud will help you do so by slowing you down. But it doesn't make much sense to try to read like this in a noisy environment: "The more noise surrounds, the harder it is to read aloud," Alan Jacobs insists. "Reading aloud, and still more *murmured* reading, requires a quiet enough environment that you can hear what you speak; otherwise it is a pointless activity."[4] Listen to the words you're reading. Let them drift around the room for a moment. No one else is listening, after all.

One of the great benefits of reading silently is that you don't have to wait for your mouth to catch up with your eyes and brain. In other words, reading silently is generally faster than reading aloud. However, the primary purpose of this book has been to demonstrate that understanding what we read—especially when what we're reading is artful—involves much more than our brains; it involves our entire selves. One of the necessary implications of the kind of reading I've discussed here is that it is slower because it requires us to read for more than information. If we need more than our brains to understand what we read, then it follows that we need to read with more than our brains. "In sacred texts, where every letter and the number of letters and their order were dictated by the godhead," Manguel notes, "full comprehension required not only the eyes but also the rest of the body: swaying to the cadence of the sentences and lifting to one's lips the holy words, so that nothing of the divine could be lost in the reading."[5] Reading aloud gets our bodies involved in the reading process, slowing us down and making us attentive to the sound and sense of the words on the page.

Sound and Sense

Slowing down to read aloud also directs our attention to the pace, tone, and direction of the words. Consider the different inflections

4. Alan Jacobs, *The Pleasures of Reading in an Age of Distraction* (New York: Oxford University Press, 2011), 119.
5. Manguel, *History of Reading*, 45–46.

with which we might speak the same sentence. For example, if you take a risk and get a gift for someone that you're not quite sure they will like, they may respond, "Oh . . . thank you." Depending on the sound, the sense of this response might be intended and interpreted in any number of ways. It could mean, "I'm genuinely grateful for this gift." Conversely, it could mean, "I don't like this gift, but I also don't want to hurt your feelings." It could mean, "I'm just not sure how to react." Or, it could mean, "Why did you get this for me?" While the recipient of the gift might say the same words in every case, their sense will be dictated by their sound.

Have you ever come to understand a passage of Scripture better after hearing it read aloud by a good reader? Perhaps it was the way a certain word or syllable was emphasized, or how the person read the verses of a psalm for the complete thought rather than pausing awkwardly at the end of lines like we do in English poems with end rhymes. Something about hearing it aloud aids in your understanding. Though the Bible was not written in English, its best translators have set out to capture not only the main ideas or thoughts of a given passage but also something of the spirit of its sound and sense. This might make for very different effects in English than it does in Hebrew, Aramaic, or Greek, but as we've seen throughout this book, the form of a text is often fundamental to its meaning. You can become a better reader of the Bible by reading it aloud because doing so teaches you to attend to how the sound of the text contributes to its sense.

We all have something the poet Robert Pinsky calls a "hearing-knowledge" of our native languages. By "hearing-knowledge," Pinsky means that kind of intuitive understanding of how words sound and work that no one ever teaches us. "The hearing-knowledge we bring to a line of poetry is a knowledge of patterns in speech we have known to hear since we were infants."[6] We learn these patterns as we learn the language. A famous example among English teachers comes from an essay by Patrick Hartwell in which he asked different groups ranging from sixth graders to first-year college students to high school teachers to present him with the grammatical rule for

6. Robert Pinsky, *The Sounds of Poetry: A Brief Guide* (New York: Farrar, Straus & Giroux, 1998), 5.

"ordering adjectives of nationality, age, and number in English. The response is always the same: 'We don't know the rule.'"[7] However, when Hartwell then gives them five words and asks them to put them in the natural order which the rule establishes, they always do so correctly. Here are the words and the order in which he gives them: "French the young girls four." "I have never seen a native speaker of English," Hartwell recounts, "who did not immediately produce the natural order, 'the four young French girls.'"[8] If you're a native English speaker, it's unlikely that anyone taught you the grammatical rule that governs the natural order of adjectives prior to learning how to put these words in order. You have a "hearing-knowledge" of English. When we read aloud, we leverage this hearing-knowledge in our attempts to enjoy and understand the text at hand.

Community

Finally, though reading aloud can be a solitary, contemplative practice, it can also be a communal event. Many Christian traditions and denominations practice the public reading of Scripture, both as an individual and a communal act. Doing so gathers the people of God together around his Word. We become satellites orbiting the Bible, our paths determined by its gravitational pull on our lives. We also hear its exhortations and admonitions together, which creates a kind of undeniable accountability to the Scriptures. Whenever the Bible is read aloud in my church, I am reminded of the fact that I cannot plead ignorance of its words. Jesus himself read the Scriptures aloud in the synagogue at the outset of his ministry. Luke 4:16–19 tells us that he came to his hometown, Nazareth, unrolled the local copy of Isaiah, and read aloud:

> The spirit of the Lord is on me,
>   because he has anointed me
>   to proclaim the good news to the poor.

7. Patrick Hartwell, "Grammar, Grammars, and the Teaching of Grammar," in *Cross-Talk in Comp Theory: A Reader*, 2nd ed., ed. Victor Villanueva (Urbana, IL: National Council of Teachers of English, 2003), 211–12.
8. Hartwell, "Grammar, Grammars," 211–12.

> He has sent me to proclaim freedom for the prisoners
> and recovery of sight for the blind,
> to set the oppressed free,
> to proclaim the year of the Lord's favor. (vv. 18–19,
>   quoting Isa. 61:1–2)

After reading the verses, he rolled the scroll back up, handed it to the attendant, and sat down with everyone still looking at him. So he said, "Today this scripture is fulfilled in your hearing" (v. 21). That's the beginning of Jesus's ministry! He reads the Scriptures aloud and fulfills them.

Though we cannot be the fulfillment of the Scriptures in the same way Jesus was, we can give them a voice. We can speak them aloud, encouraging our brothers and sisters and following in the footsteps of Jesus. We can give the very words of life to each other as gifts from God. The very act of reading aloud is itself an act of love.

Bibliography

Abrams, M. H. *The Mirror and the Lamp*. Oxford: Oxford University Press, 1971.

Alighieri, Dante. *The Divine Comedy*. Translated by John Ciardi. New York: New American Library, 2003.

Alter, Robert. *The Art of Biblical Poetry*. New York: Basic Books, 1985. Revised and updated, 2011.

———. *The Pleasures of Reading in an Ideological Age*. New York: Simon & Schuster, 1989.

Aristotle. *Nicomachean Ethics*. Translated by Terence Irwin. 2nd ed. Indianapolis: Hackett, 1999.

———. *Poetics*. Translated by Malcolm Heath. New York: Penguin, 1996.

Augustine. *Confessions*. Translated by F. J. Sheed. 2nd ed. Indianapolis: Hackett, 2006.

———. *On Christian Teaching*. Translated by R. P. H. Green. New York: Oxford University Press, 2008.

Beckett, Samuel. "Dante . . . Bruno . . . Vico . . . Joyce." In *Disjecta: Miscellaneous Writings and a Dramatic Fragment; Samuel Beckett*, edited by Ruby Cohn, 18–33. New York: Grove Press, 1984.

Berlin, Adele. *The Dynamics of Biblical Parallelism*. Rev. ed. Grand Rapids: Eerdmans, 2008. First published 1985 by Indiana University Press (Bloomington).

Bonhoeffer, Dietrich. *Psalms: The Prayer Book of the Bible*. Minneapolis: Augsburg Fortress, 1974.

Bradstreet, Anne. "The Author to Her Book." Poetry Foundation. Accessed March 12, 2020. https://www.poetryfoundation.org/poems/43697/the -author-to-her-book.

Braithwaite, William Stanley. "The Negro in American Literature." In *Within the Circle: An Anthology of African American Literary Criticism from the Harlem Renaissance to the Present*, edited by Angelyn Mitchell, 32–44. Durham, NC: Duke University Press, 1994.

Braxton, Joanne M. "Paul Laurence Dunbar." In *The Concise Oxford Companion to African American Literature*, edited by William L. Andrews, Frances Smith Foster, and Trudier Harris, 119–20. New York: Oxford University Press, 2001.

Brooks, Cleanth. "The Heresy of Paraphrase." In *The Well Wrought Urn*, 192–214. New York: Harcourt, Brace, 1975.

Brueggemann, Walter. "Biblical Authority: A Personal Reflection." In *Struggling with Scripture*, edited by William Sloane Coffin, 5–31. Louisville: Westminster John Knox, 2002.

Cervantes, Miguel de. *Don Quixote*. Translated by John Rutherford. New York: Penguin, 2003.

Chopin, Kate. "Désirée's Baby." In *The Awakening, and Other Stories*, 204–10. Cambridge: Cambridge University Press, 1996.

Ciardi, John, and Miller Williams. *How Does a Poem Mean?* 2nd ed. Boston: Houghton Mifflin, 1975.

Collins, Billy. "Introduction to Poetry." In *The Apple That Astonished Paris*, 58. Fayetteville: University of Arkansas Press, 1988.

Cosper, Mike. *Rhythms of Grace: How the Church's Worship Tells the Story of the Gospel*. Wheaton: Crossway, 2013.

Costen, Melva Wilson. *African American Christian Worship*. 2nd ed. Nashville: Abingdon, 2007.

Crainshaw, Jill Y. "Embodied Remembering: Wisdom, Character, and Worship." In *Character & Scripture: Moral Formation, Community, and Biblical Interpretation*, edited by William P. Brown, 363–88. Grand Rapids: Eerdmans, 2002.

Culler, Jonathan. *Theory of the Lyric*. Cambridge, MA: Harvard University Press, 2015.

Dickinson, Emily. *Poems*. Edited by Mabel Loomis Todd and T. W. Higginson. Boston: Little, Brown, 1902.

Dobbs-Allsopp, F. W. *On Biblical Poetry*. New York: Oxford University Press, 2015.

Du Bois, W. E. B. *The Souls of Black Folk*. New York: Penguin, 2009.

Dunbar, Paul Laurence. "We Wear the Mask." Poetry Foundation. Accessed March 12, 2020. https://www.poetryfoundation.org/poems/44203/we -wear-the-mask.

Eagleton, Terry. *How to Read a Poem*. Malden, MA: Blackwell, 2007.

———. *How to Read Literature*. New Haven: Yale University Press, 2013.

Eliot, T. S. "Tradition and the Individual Talent." In *Selected Essays*, 3–11. New York: Harcourt, Brace, 1950.

———. *The Waste Land*. Poetry Foundation. Accessed February 13, 2020. https://www.poetryfoundation.org/poems/47311/the-waste-land.

Emanuel, James A. "Racial Fire in the Poetry of Paul Laurence Dunbar." In *A Singer in the Dawn: Reinterpretations of Paul Laurence Dunbar*, edited by Jay Martin, 75–93. New York: Dodd, Mead, 1975.

Emerson, Ralph Waldo. *Selected Essays of Emerson*. Edited by Larzer Ziff. New York: Penguin, 2003.

Felski, Rita. *Uses of Literature*. Malden, MA: Blackwell, 2008.

Flaubert, Gustave. *Madame Bovary*. New York: Random House, 1991.

Foer, Jonathan Safran. *Extremely Loud and Incredibly Close*. Boston: Mariner, 2005.

Fokkelman, J. P. *Reading Biblical Poetry: An Introductory Guide*. Louisville: Westminster John Knox, 2001.

Foster, Richard J. *Celebration of Discipline: The Path to Spiritual Growth*. Rev. ed. Downers Grove, IL: InterVarsity, 1988.

Frost, Robert. "Birches." Poets.org. Academy of American Poets. Accessed February 13, 2020. https://poets.org/poem/birches.

———. "The Road Not Taken." Poets.org. Academy of American Poets. Accessed February 13, 2020. https://poets.org/poem/road-not-taken.

Gadamer, Hans-Georg. *Truth and Method*. Revised translation by Joel Weinsheimer and Donald G. Marshall. New York: Bloomsbury T&T Clark, 2013.

Gay, Ross. *The Book of Delights: Essays*. Chapel Hill, NC: Algonquin Books, 2019.

Hamilton, Sharon. *Essential Literary Terms: A Brief Norton Guide with Exercises*. New York: Norton, 2007.

Harper, Frances Ellen Watkins. "Eliza Harris." *Liberator*, December 16, 1853.

Hartwell, Patrick. "Grammar, Grammars, and the Teaching of Grammar." In *Cross-Talk in Comp Theory: A Reader*, edited by Victor Villanueva, 2nd ed., 205–33. Urbana, IL: National Council of Teachers of English, 2003.

Hewitt, Rachel. *A Revolution of Feeling: The Decade That Forged the Modern Mind*. London: Granta, 2017.

Honoré, Carl. *In Praise of Slowness: Challenging the Cult of Speed*. New York: HarperCollins, 2005.

Ingraham, Christopher. "Poetry Is Going Extinct, Government Data Show." *Washington Post*, April 24, 2015, https://www.washingtonpost.com/news/wonk/wp/2015/04/24/poetry-is-going-extinct-government-data -show/.

Jacobs, Alan. *The Pleasures of Reading in an Age of Distraction*. New York: Oxford University Press, 2011.

———. *A Theology of Reading: The Hermeneutics of Love*. New York: Westview, 2001.

Johnson, Thomas H., ed. *The Complete Poems of Emily Dickinson*. Boston: Little, Brown, 1960.

Keats, John. "A Letter to George and Thomas Keats." In *The Critical Tradition: Classic Texts and Contemporary Trends*, edited by David H. Richter, 320. New York: St. Martin's Press, 1989.

Klinkenborg, Verlyn. *Several Short Sentences about Writing*. New York: Vintage, 2012.

Kugel, James. *The Idea of Biblical Poetry*. New Haven: Yale University Press, 1981.

Lerner, Ben. *The Hatred of Poetry*. New York: Farrar, Straus & Giroux, 2016.

Lewis, C. S. *Reflections on the Psalms*. 1958. Reprint, New York: HarperOne, 2017.

Logan, William. "Against Aesthetics." *New Criterion* 32, no. 1 (September 2013): 20–24.

Longman, Tremper, III. *How to Read the Psalms*. Downers Grove, IL: InterVarsity, 1988.

Luther, Martin. "Psalm 117." Translated by Edward Sittler. In *Luther's Works*, vol. 14, *Selected Psalms III*, edited by Jaroslav Pelikan, 1–39. St. Louis: Concordia, 1958.

Manguel, Alberto. *A History of Reading*. New York: Viking, 1996.

Marx, William. *The Hatred of Literature*. Translated by Nicholas Elliott. Cambridge, MA: Belknap, 2018.

McGrath, Thomas. "Language, Power, and Dream." In *Claims for Poetry*, edited by Donald Hall, 286–95. Ann Arbor: University of Michigan Press, 1982.

McKay, Claude. *Harlem Shadows: The Poems of Claude McKay*. New York: Harcourt, Brace, 1922.

Moore, Marianne. "Poetry." In *Complete Poems*, 36. New York: Penguin, 1994.

Nussbaum, Martha C. *Love's Knowledge: Essays on Philosophy and Literature*. New York: Oxford University Press, 1990.

Oliver, Mary. *A Poetry Handbook*. New York: Harcourt, Brace, 1994.

Peterson, Eugene. *Eat This Book: A Conversation in the Art of Spiritual Reading*. Grand Rapids: Eerdmans, 2006.

Phillips, Carl. *Coin of the Realm: Essays on the Life and Art of Poetry*. St. Paul: Graywolf, 2004.

Pinsky, Robert. *The Sounds of Poetry: A Brief Guide*. New York: Farrar, Straus & Giroux, 1998.

Plato. *Apology*. In *Plato: Complete Works*, edited by John M. Cooper, 17–36. Indianapolis: Hackett, 1997.

———. *Republic*. In *Plato: Complete Works*, edited by John M. Cooper, 371–1223. Indianapolis: Hackett, 1997.

Prior, Karen Swallow. *On Reading Well: Finding the Good Life through Great Books*. Grand Rapids: Brazos, 2018.

Raabe, Paul R. "Deliberate Ambiguity in the Psalter." *Journal of Biblical Literature* 110, no. 2 (Summer 1991): 213–27.

Robbins, Michael. *Equipment for Living: On Poetry and Pop Music*. New York: Simon & Schuster, 2017.

Rukeyser, Muriel. *The Life of Poetry*. Ashfield, MA: Paris Press, 1996.

Ryken, Leland. *Words of Delight: A Literary Introduction to the Bible*. Grand Rapids: Baker, 1992.

Schmemann, Alexander. *For the Life of the World*. Crestwood, NY: St. Vladimir's Seminary Press, 1963.

Scott, Temple. *The Pleasure of Reading the Bible*. New York: Mitchell Kennerley, 1909.

Shklovsky, Viktor. "Art as Technique." In *The Critical Tradition: Classic Texts and Contemporary Trends*, edited by David H. Richter, 738–48. New York: St. Martin's Press, 1989.

Smith, James K. A. *Desiring the Kingdom: Worship, Worldview, and Cultural Formation.* Cultural Liturgies 1. Grand Rapids: Baker Academic, 2009.

———. *You Are What You Love: The Spiritual Power of Habit.* Grand Rapids: Brazos, 2016.

Sontag, Susan. *Against Interpretation, and Other Essays.* New York: Picador, 2001.

Steiner, George. *Real Presences.* Chicago: University of Chicago Press, 1989.

Sutherland, John. *How Literature Works: 50 Key Concepts.* New York: Oxford University Press, 2011.

Tanselle, Thomas. "The Thomas Seltzer Imprint." *Papers of the Bibliographical Society of America* 58, no. 4 (Fourth Quarter 1964): 380–448.

Thackrey, Donald E. *Emily Dickinson's Approach to Poetry.* University of Nebraska Studies. Lincoln, NE: Folcroft Library Editions, 1973.

Thiselton, Anthony. *The Two Horizons: New Testament Hermeneutics and Philosophical Description.* Grand Rapids: Eerdmans, 1980.

Thomas, Frank A. *They Like to Never Quit Praisin' God: The Role of Celebration in Preaching.* Cleveland: United Church Press, 1997.

Tolkien, J. R. R. *The Fellowship of the Ring.* New York: Ballantine, 2012.

Travers, Michael E. *Encountering God in the Psalms.* Grand Rapids: Kregel, 2003.

Vendler, Helen. "Author's Notes for Teaching *Poems, Poets, Poetry.*" In *Poems, Poets, Poetry: An Introduction and Anthology*, edited by Helen Vendler, 3rd ed., 1–98. New York: St. Martin's Press, 2010.

Wainwright, Geoffrey. "Christian Worship: Scriptural Basis and Theological Frame." In *The Oxford History of Christian Worship*, edited by Geoffrey Wainwright and Karen B. Westerfield Tucker, 1–31. New York: Oxford University Press, 2006.

Wallace, David Foster, and Larry McCaffery. "An Expanded Interview with David Foster Wallace." In *Conversations with David Foster Wallace*, edited by Stephen J. Burn, 21–52. Jackson: University Press of Mississippi, 2012.

Warren, Tish Harrison. *Liturgy of the Ordinary: Sacred Practices in Everyday Life.* Downers Grove, IL: InterVarsity, 2016.

Wordsworth, William. "Preface to *Lyrical Ballads.*" In *The Critical Tradition: Classic Texts and Contemporary Trends*, edited by David H. Richter, 285–98. New York: St. Martin's Press, 1989.

Zapruder, Matthew. *Why Poetry.* New York: Ecco, 2017.

Index